The lull before the storm: Bathonians going about their daily business in Southgate Street during the late 1930s. How many of them could foresee the carnage soon to be unleashed on their defenceless city?

BATH
AT WAR
1939–1945

DAVID AND JONATHAN FALCONER

SUTTON PUBLISHING

with *The* **Bath Chronicle**

First published in the United Kingdom in 1999 by
Sutton Publishing Limited · Phoenix Mill
Thrupp · Stroud · Gloucestershire · GL5 2BU
with *The Bath Chronicle*

British Library Cataloguing in Publication Data
A catalogue record for this book is available from the British Library

ISBN 0 7509 1995 7

Dedication
This book is dedicated to the memory of Bath's war dead, killed on
the Home Front or while serving with the Forces during the Second
World War.

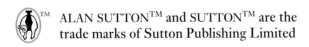 ALAN SUTTON™ and SUTTON™ are the
trade marks of Sutton Publishing Limited

Typeset in 11/12pt Ehrhardt.
Typesetting and origination by
Sutton Publishing Limited.
Printed in Great Britain by
Ebenezer Baylis, Worcester.

Contents

Acknowledgements

The authors would like to thank the following individuals and organisations for their help in the preparation of this book:

Catherine Alley; Barbara Bigwood; Frank Brown; Philip Comm DCM; Ione Denny; Reg Gray; Paul Lashmar; Phyllis Miles; John Penny for so kindly allowing us to quote from his unpublished MA dissertation about the bombing of Bath in 1942; Bob White for help with details of Bath City FC's activities during the war.

David Ashby, Ministry of Defence Naval Historical Branch, London; Stuart Burroughs, Bath Industrial Heritage Centre; the Commonwealth War Graves Commission, Marlow; Liz Bevan, Bath Central Library, for help in obtaining photographs from the Bath Reference Library collections, and for kind permission to reproduce them in this book; Colin Johnston, Bath City Archivist; Robin Stewart of the Kingsmead Motor Company, Bath, for kindly allowing us to reproduce the photograph of the Ford emergency food van; David Gledhill and Katy Lee, *The Bath Chronicle*, for their support; Bath Rotary Club, Alison Wells and Edward Barrett of Bath & North East Somerset Council, for their valued assistance with the Alkmaar story. And last but not least, Clare Bishop, Anne Bennett, Michelle Tilling and Rupert Harding at Sutton Publishing for all their help.

Few photographs from the *Chronicle* archives of wartime Bath have survived into the late twentieth century. For the purposes of this publication, it has been necessary in some instances to make copies direct from wartime issues of the newspaper. The quality of these images is not good, but they have been included for their interest value and because no other copies exist. All photographs are from the *Chronicle* archives unless credited otherwise.

That wartime spirit: two nights of bombing failed to disrupt the rhythm of daily life in wartime Bath as these two housewives demonstrate.

Introduction

Without a doubt the Second World War in general, and the Bath blitz in particular, wrought more far-reaching changes on Bath than any event in its long and colourful history. So far no one has written a book that looks at all aspects of the city's life during the Second World War and how its citizens coped. This is the first to do so.

In a book of this size the picture we paint of the City of Bath at war between 1939 and 1945 is necessarily a broad one. Many local people today know of the blitz in April 1942, which to date has received comparatively widespread coverage on television, in books and in the local press – and quite rightly so, because it caused such extensive suffering and devastation in the city. We have chosen to look at Bath's war from a thematic viewpoint, rather than simply telling the story of the war as it unfolded through a chronological narrative. The reason for this approach is that we can thereby concentrate in depth on a particular activity, for example food rationing, rather than present to the reader a string of disparate references dotted throughout the book. In a way, these themes can be viewed as snapshots of city life, highlighting some of the important events that defined its war and that of its inhabitants, both directly and indirectly. As well as the more earth-shattering events of the war, we have also included details of some seemingly trivial occurrences that took place in Bath, but which none the less assumed importance in the everyday lives of many Bathonians.

Our principal source of material has been the wartime editions of the *Bath and Wilts Chronicle and Herald*, Bath's evening newspaper, which also covered north and mid-Somerset, Wiltshire and south Gloucestershire. In more than 2,000 issues there are rich seams of news reports, editorial comment and photographs that describe and illustrate the daily effects of the war on Bath, and how its citizens rose to meet the great challenge. We have delved into the archives of the wartime *Chronicle* to help compile this book, and its reports form the basis of much of what you are about to read. Published by Wessex Associated News Ltd from their offices at 33 Westgate Street, the *Chronicle* prided itself on never missing a single issue throughout the entire war, despite bomb damage to the printing works and editorial offices that put the Westgate Street premises out of action for the best part of a month following the blitz.

Newspapers in wartime Britain were an important part of the people's daily lives. According to the government's *Wartime Social Survey*, four in five men and two in three women saw a newspaper on any one day during the war. The year 1943 saw newspaper consumption in Britain reach a wartime high with more copies bought per head of population than before the war. Not only did they provide a detailed digest of news upon which people could reflect and form an opinion, newspapers also entertained with advertisements, cartoons and puzzles. But despite the rush to produce a newspaper and get it on to the news stands, once read they were – and still are – discarded more quickly than almost any other product.

The popular belief that 'I read it in the paper, therefore it must be true' became even less credible during the war years when official censorship of news stories and photographs was rife. Under emergency regulation, the Government could close down a newspaper in a matter of hours if it was found guilty of 'obtaining, recording, communicating to any other person or publishing information which

might be useful to an enemy'. Quite obviously the Government wanted to make sure the public was kept informed of the news to avoid the danger of rumours spreading, but understandably did not want thoughtless reporting of war news in British newspapers. Publishing details of the results of enemy bombing raids on Britain, or the whereabouts of a particular factory in a certain town that was manufacturing munitions, clearly would act as a free information service to German intelligence. Editors were presented with a copy of a document known as the Defence Notices (more commonly referred to as D–Notices) that listed subjects about which it was considered that no information should be published without first seeking advice from the censor. Essentially, the censorship of newspapers remained voluntary and most editors were enlightened enough to cooperate.

Occasionally some of the facts and interpretations contained in the wartime *Chronicle* are not entirely correct, but we should stop and consider that the men and women who wrote, edited and printed the paper did so under the constraints described above, without knowing if tomorrow would ever come, or indeed who in the end would win the war. But more importantly for us today, we should view Bath's local newspaper as a priceless chronicle of history as it was being made, and we owe a debt of thanks to those largely nameless men and women who worked such long hours in very uncertain times to ensure we were kept informed.

We hope that what you are about to read will reveal just how much the Second World War was the people's war. The bombing of Bath brought the war literally into people's front rooms, and the rationing of almost every commodity from clothing to foodstuffs ensured that most citizens were acutely aware of their personal involvement in the fight against Hitler. Our book also shows the vast amount of official interference in the lives of ordinary people; at no other time in history have the people of Britain suffered such draconian restrictions of their personal freedom as they did between 1939 and 1945.

The sad conclusion to this story is that although we may have won the war in 1945, as a nation we certainly lost the peace.

David Falconer, Trowbridge
Jonathan Falconer, Bradford-on-Avon
October 1998

Chronology

1939
September
1   Germany invades Poland.
3   Britain and France declare war on Germany.
October
1/2   RAF Whitley bomber becomes first British aircraft of the war to fly over Berlin.
14   British battleship HMS *Royal Oak* sunk at Scapa Flow by German *U-47*.
December
17   German pocket battleship *Graf Spee* scuttled in Uruguayan waters off Montevideo.

1940
April
9   German forces invade Denmark and Norway.
May
10   German forces invade the Low Countries. Churchill replaces Chamberlain as Premier and forms National Government.
26 May– Evacuation of 336,000 Allied troops from
4 June Dunkirk.
June
10   Italy declares war on Britain and France.
14   Paris falls to German forces.
17   France sues for peace.
July
10   Battle of Britain begins.
August
24/25 First German bombs fall on central London.
September
13   Italy invades Egypt.
October
31   Battle of Britain ends.
November
11/12 Swordfish aircraft of the Royal Navy attack and severely damage Italian fleet at Taranto.
14/15 Devastating German attack on Coventry by 457 German bombers kills 568 people.
15   Germany seals off Jews in Warsaw ghetto.

1941
January
22   Tobruk falls to British Army.
February
12   Rommel invades Libya.
March
28   Royal Navy wins victory over Italian fleet at Battle of Cape Matapan.
May
11   Rudolph Hess, Hitler's deputy, parachutes into Scotland.
24   HMS *Hood* sunk by German battleship *Bismarck*.
27   *Bismarck* sunk.
28–31 British forces evacuate Crete.
June
22   German forces invade Russia.
July
5   German troops reach Dniepr.
September
9   Siege of Leningrad begins.
19   Germans take Kiev.
October
2 Oct.– Battle of Moscow.
5 Dec.

November
18 Nov.– German–Italian forces retreat
30 Dec. before British 8th Army in N. Africa.
December
5   Soviet counter-offensive launched.
7   Japanese bombers launch an unprovoked attack on US naval base at Pearl Harbor.
8   Japanese forces invade Thailand and Malaya.
8/9   Britain, the Commonwealth countries, the USA and China unite to declare war on Japan.
10   HMS *Prince of Wales* and *Repulse* sunk by Japanese aircraft.
11   Germany and Italy declare war on USA.
16   Germans retreat along Moscow front.
25   Hong Kong surrenders to Japanese.

1942
January
16   Japanese begin Burma offensive.
20   Germans discuss 'Final solution of Jewish question'.
21   Rommel launches last German offensive in Libya.
February
12   'Channel Dash' – the German warships *Scharnhorst*, *Gneisenau* and *Prinz Eugen* sail from Brest to Germany through the Dover Straits. Attempts to stop them by 242 RAF bomber aircraft fail.
15   Singapore falls to Japanese forces.
27   Japanese defeat Allied naval force in Battle of the Java Sea.
April
23–27 Rostock raided by RAF on four consecutive nights.
25–27 Bath raided by German bombers on two consecutive nights, 400 killed.
May
30/31 First 1,000-bomber raid when RAF attack Cologne.
June
1/2   Second 1,000-bomber raid, target Essen.
3–7   Battle of Midway, decisive US air and naval victory over Japanese.
July
2–4   First Battle of El Alamein, decisive blow to Rommel.
August
19   Disastrous Anglo–Canadian raid on Dieppe.
September
6   Battle of Stalingrad begins.
October
23 Oct.– Montgomery launches successful offensive at
4 Nov. El Alamein.
November
12–15 Japanese Navy defeated by US at Guadalcanal.

1943
January
14–24 Casablanca Conference attended by Churchill and Roosevelt decides to accept nothing short of unconditional German and Japanese surrender.
31   German 6th Army surrenders at Stalingrad. Hitler's Russian offensive collapses.

April
7   British 8th Army and US 1st Army link up in Tunisia.
May
16/17   'Dambuster' Lancasters of the RAF's 617 Squadron attack Germany's Ruhr dams.
July
24 July–   Hamburg attacked on 4 nights, huge civilian
3 Aug.   casualties from resulting firestorm.

August
17   US–British capture of Messina ends German resistance in Sicily.
September
9   Allied invasion of Italy. Italian Army surrenders.
October
13   Italy declares war on Germany.
November
6   Kiev liberated from Germans.
December
26   German battlecruiser *Scharnhorst* sunk by Royal Navy.

1944
January
24   US General Eisenhower appointed Supreme Commander of Allied Forces in Europe.
February
14   German siege of Leningrad lifted.
15   Monte Cassino bombed.
March
30/31   RAF's biggest loss of the war, target Nuremberg. 795 aircraft despatched, 95 lost.
May
18   British take Cassino, Poles take Monte Cassino.
June
4   Allies enter Rome.
6   D–Day, Allies land in Normandy. The biggest seaborne invasion in history.
13   Germans launch first V1 Flying Bombs against England.
July
9   British troops take Caen.
20   Failed assassination attempt on Hitler.
August
24   Paris liberated.
September
17   British airborne operation to capture Rhine bridges at Arnhem fails.
25   Hitler mobilises all men between the ages of sixteen and sixty into *Volksturm*.
October
24–26   US forces defeat Japanese fleet at Leyte.
November
12   German battleship *Tirpitz* sunk by RAF bombers in Tromsö Fjord.
December
16   German offensive opens in the Ardennes – the 'Battle of the Bulge'.

1945
January
14–18   Soviet Army captures Warsaw.
26   Ardennes completely liberated.

27   Soviets liberate Auschwitz concentration camp.
February
13   US 1st Army crosses the Rhine.
14/15   Dresden bombed by RAF and USAAF. Terrific firestorm kills over 135,000.
19   US Marines land on Iwo Jima.
20/21   The first of thirty-six consecutive night raids on Berlin by RAF Mosquito bombers.
March
1–6   Monchengladbach, Krefeld, Treves and Cologne fall to US forces.
12   1,108 RAF aircraft bomb Dortmund in the largest raid of the whole war.
16   US Marines take Iwo Jima.
20   Anglo–Indian forces take Mandalay in Burma.
23   British and US troops under Montgomery cross Rhine between Rees and Wesel.
28   Collapse of German Army in the West.
April
1   Twenty-one German divisions encircled in the Ruhr.
12   US President Roosevelt dies. Truman succeeds him.
13   Soviet Army takes Vienna.
16   Ground battle for Berlin begins.
26   US and Soviet troops in historic link-up at Torgau on the Elbe. Bremen surrenders to British.
29 Apr.– Operation 'Manna' – food supplies dropped
7 May   to the starving people of Holland by the RAF and USAAF.
30   Hitler commits suicide in Berlin bunker.
May
2   Berlin surrenders to Soviet Army. Australians land on Borneo.
3   Anglo–Indian forces take Rangoon and Prome.
7   Unconditional surrender of all German forces to the Allies.
8   VE–Day.
July
5   General MacArthur announces liberation of Philippines.
26   US, Britain and China send ultimatum to Japan. Labour party wins British general election. Churchill resigns.
27   Attlee forms new government.
28   Tokyo rejects ultimatum.
August
2   British liberate Burma.
6   Atomic bomb dropped on Hiroshima.
9   Atomic bomb dropped on Nagasaki.
15   VJ–Day. Japan formally announces surrender.
29   American forces begin occupation of Japan.
November
20   War crimes trials open before international tribunal in Nuremberg.

1946
3 May   War crimes trials open before international tribunal in Tokyo.

CHAPTER 1

'If You Want Peace, Prepare For War'

With the end of the 'war to end all wars' in 1918, Germany was forced to accept full guilt for starting the war and a punitive peace settlement by the victorious powers of Britain, France and America. It was based on occupation, dismemberment and disarmament, and the payment of huge sums of money in reparations for the devastation Germany had caused. But even as the Peace of Versailles was being drafted in 1919, it was clear to many that the problem of German militarism would never disappear.

With the horrors of the First World War now put behind them, the people of Britain tried hard to forget the suffering it had brought them and got on with living their lives as best they could. But politicians at home and abroad failed to grasp the fact that the vindictive nature of the peace terms would sooner or later lead to more trouble. It was a matter of when and not if Germany would rise again to right the wrongs she felt had been forced on her.

Marshal Foch, one of France's great military leaders of the First World War, had warned his countrymen prophetically in 1919: 'This is not a peace; it is an Armistice for twenty years'. And time was to prove him right.

In the Germany of the 1920s resentment was beginning to boil over. With a fast-growing social and economic crisis, Weimar Germany was in a mess and the conditions were right for a new leader to step out from the shadows. His name was Adolf Hitler. In January 1933 President Hindenburg appointed Hitler chancellor and with the Reichstag elections in March he and his Nazi party swept to power, although they had won only 44 per cent of the vote. Hitler proceeded to smash Weimar institutions and all possible sources of resistance to Nazism, forging the new Nazi state under his absolute control. In the years that followed, Hitler put Germany back on its feet, restored national pride and embarked on a programme of rapid industrial and military growth. He also looked beyond Germany's borders with a view to colonial expansion.

Thanks to the feebleness of the League of Nations and the mood of appeasement in Europe that desired peace at any price, Hitler was able to ignore the terms of the Peace of Versailles because he had shrewdly gambled on the world standing by, afraid to do anything. He set about building an army, a navy and an air force that were soon capable of world domination. Meanwhile, the British Government continued to reduce the strength of our armed forces.

Throughout the 1930s Britons got on with their lives, but still cast the occasional glance over their shoulders to watch the rise to power of Adolf Hitler in Germany. Some were astute enough to realise that another war was brewing and that Britain must be prepared should it finally come.

On 13 March 1938 German troops marched into Austria, merging it with Germany in what became known as the *Anschluss* or 'union'. In early September

A prewar scene at the bottom of Milsom Street.

Hitler demanded the annexation of the Czech Sudetenland to Germany and an intense war scare gripped Europe when Czechoslovakia refused to comply. Chamberlain, Daladier, Mussolini and Hitler met in Munich on 29 September to discuss the Sudetenland crisis. They offered Hitler all he wanted in the belief that this would be the last of his demands for European territory with a German-majority population. The Prime Minister, Neville Chamberlain, returned to London from his meeting with Herr Hitler, clutching the famous piece of paper and uttering the immortal words: 'I believe it is peace for our time'.

Munich was a sell-out to Hitler, the nascent bully of Europe, and proved to him that if he pushed hard enough any potential adversary would cave in to his demands. But it also gave Britain a much needed breathing space, time to speed up rearmament and prepare for a war that by now seemed unavoidable. When Germany invaded the rest of Czechoslovakia in March 1939, it became clear to even the most doubting observers that Hitler meant business. But where would he strike next? As the storm clouds of war began to gather over Europe in the summer of 1939, the City of Bath made the first of its preparations for the inevitable conflict soon to come.

On the night of Saturday 8 July a 'feigned state of emergency', much publicised in the *Chronicle*, gripped the city. By means of an imaginary air raid, its aim was to test the efficiency and response of Bath's air raid precautions personnel and fighter squadrons of the RAF. On the Thursday before the event, the *Chronicle* had reported on its front pages that:

From midnight on Saturday to 4 o'clock on Sunday morning there will be a feigned state of emergency in Somerset, Wiltshire, Gloucestershire and Dorset.

. . . A personnel of at least 1,500 will be engaged. The 'narrative' which produces the black-out is dramatically worded, being to the following effect:

'An imaginary acute tension exists throughout Europe, brought about by political conflicts and movement of troops of the Central Powers in Eastern Europe. On July 2nd the British government as a precautionary measure decided to declare a state of emergency. Respirators were issued and the evacuation scheme put into effect. On July 6th hostile aerial raids were made on London and several Midland towns . . .'.

At midnight on the 8th, Bath's air raid sirens wailed out their chilling call that a black-out under wartime conditions had started. It lasted until 4 a.m. when the All Clear was sounded by a two-minute long steady note on the siren. As dawn broke on the morning of the 9th, the city authorities congratulated themselves on the great success of the black-out, and the headlines in Monday's *Chronicle* echoed their satisfaction:

Bath's Great Black-out a Success
Hundreds, if not thousands, of people in Bath came out – or stayed out – to see what the city would look like in total darkness. They stood about in the streets and waited for the intermittent blasts of the sirens which denoted zero hour. The sirens sounded and after that there were few lights to be seen. An occasional illuminated sign caught the eye. An occasional car passed with lights fully aglow, but the majority of motor vehicles conformed with the request that side lamps only should be alight and that they should be covered with blue paper.

Excavations for a public air raid shelter in Queen Square. By July 1939 the city authorities had spent £7,295 on eleven public shelters, with more to come.

Left: Cater, Stoffell & Fortt ('The Stores') advertisement in the Chronicle *for air raid precautions equipment.* Above*: Preparing for the black-out: a tree in Pulteney Street receives bands of white paint in August 1939 to make it more conspicuous to pedestrians and motorists.*

Measures to protect the citizens of Bath from the threat of air raids and contingency plans for wartime food control in the city continued apace throughout July and into August. Finishing touches were put to air raid shelters that had been hastily started during the Munich Crisis a year before and then forgotten after the Prime Minister, Neville Chamberlain's triumphal return:

So far a sum of £7,295 has been spent on building air-raid shelters in eleven different parts of Bath. These will accommodate 1,683 persons, but before they can be said to be entirely ready a further £1,870 is to be spent – as far as possible – on making them 'more homely', by providing seating accommodation etc.

The *Chronicle* of 31 August revealed how one company in Bath displayed particular enthusiasm in ensuring that its employees were well practised in air raid precautions:

Most Bath business concerns of any size have completed their air-raid precautions and many of them have held rehearsals. At the premises of Messrs Duck, Son & Pinker, Bridge Street, this morning, buzzers sounded a warning. In less than three minutes the 48 members of the indoor staff were under cover. . . . The cellars used as shelters are electrically lighted and provided with seating. Candles in piano sconces are fixed round the walls and will be used in the event of any electrical breakdown.

Throughout August the *Chronicle* had carried dozens of photographs of Bath's emergency preparations for a war that many now saw as inevitable. A list of the whereabouts of public shelters and air raid trenches was printed in the paper on 29 August. On the city's streets white bands were painted on trees and broad white lines painted down the middle of the roads to help pedestrians and motorists find their way in the blackout. Traffic lights and car headlamps were fitted with shrouds to dim their lights. Gas masks, assembled and packed by an army of volunteers from local firms, were distributed:

> Distribution of gas masks will be completed within a few days. Seventy thousand of them have been assembled and packed in cartons at the stores at James Street West and Frome Road House during the past week and the ARP authorities in the city are anxious that the public should realise the importance of looking after the respirators.

A sense of almost comical self-delusion appeared to colour some reports in the *Chronicle* as frantic last-ditch efforts were made behind the scenes on the international stage to avert war, and the last few days of peace ticked away almost unnoticed. The huge white letters 'BATH', that for many years had graced the top a gasometer on the Upper Bristol Road as a navigational guide to passing aircraft, had been hastily painted out the previous year during the Munich Crisis. In August 1939 the *Chronicle* thought this measure sufficient to disguise the identity of the city from

GAS MASKS

With frightening memories of the battlefields of the First World War still fresh in the minds of the older generation, preparations were made some time before the outbreak of the Second World War to safeguard the civilian population in case Hitler decided to use poison gas against Britain in air attacks. With the scare of the Munich Crisis in September 1938, some 38 million gas masks were hurriedly distributed to every household in the country.

Gas masks were carried in brown cardboard cartons. The rubber masks were designed for use by adults and young children. For very young children a special mask was designed that looked like Mickey Mouse and which was intended to be less frightening for them. At first nothing was available that would be suitable for babies, but these were supplied later in the form of macabre-looking gas helmets.

Bath's ARP wardens made a point of checking young children's masks every three months so that those who had reached the age of four or four-and-a-half could exchange their Mickey Mouse masks for larger ones.

Fortunately, poison gas was never used during the Second World War, although there were occasions when it seemed likely and at such times people made a point of taking their respirators everywhere with them.

PRACTISE PUTTING ON YOUR RESPIRATOR

1. Hold your breath. (*To inhale gas may be fatal.*) 2. Hold mask in front of face, thumbs inside straps. 3. Thrust chin well forward into mask. Pull straps as far over head as they will go. 4. Run finger round face-piece taking care head-straps are not twisted.

MAKE SURE IT FITS

See that the rubber fits snugly at sides of jaw and under chin. The head-straps should be adjusted so that they hold the mask firmly on the face. To test for fit, hold a piece of soft, flat rubber or of soft tissue paper to end of mask and breathe in. The rubber or paper should stick.

Arrows indicate points needing particular attention.

The possibility of gas attacks was taken seriously. Gas masks (respirators) were issued to all adults and children at the time of the Munich Crisis in 1938. In 1942 the Ministry of Home Security issued a Chart of War Gases for the guidance of civilians, together with instructions for putting on respirators. Frequent practice was recommended. (Authors)

N.R. 50.

NATIONAL **REGISTER.**

NATIONAL REGISTRATION DAY IS FRIDAY, 29th SEPTEMBER, 1939.

SEE INSTRUCTIONS IN SCHEDULE AS TO "PERSONS TO BE INCLUDED."

RATIONING.—The return on the schedule herewith will be used not only for National Registration but also for Food Rationing purposes. It is to your interest, therefore, as well as your public duty, to fill up the return carefully, fully and accurately.

Help the Enumerator to collect the schedule promptly by arranging for him to receive it when he calls. Do not make it necessary for him to call a number of times before he can obtain it.

When the Enumerator collects the schedule, he must write and deliver an Identity Card for every person included in the return. Help him to write them properly for you by letting him write at a table.

If the whole household moves before the schedule is collected, take it with you and hand it to the Enumerator calling at your new residence or to the National Registration Office for your new address. The address of this office can be ascertained at a local police station.

Wt 28033—171 12 50

An official communique distributed to all households in the city giving notice of National Registration Day on Friday 29 September 1939. Registration was required for the issue of ration books and identity cards. (Authors)

the air and to prevent its location by German bombers. A report on 31 August declared that 'Bath is not likely to have any Anderson air-raid shelters as it is a non-vulnerable area. These will probably only be supplied if and when the area becomes a vulnerable one.' Sadly, time was to prove the fallacy of these arguments.

German tanks rolled across Poland's borders on 1 September in a blatant act of aggression. At 9 a.m. on Sunday 3 September Britain's Ambassador to Berlin, Sir Nevile Henderson, arrived at an eerily deserted German Foreign Office in the Wilhemlstrasse, where he read an ultimatum from His Majesty's Government to Hitler's interpreter, demanding the immediate withdrawal of German forces from Poland.

A thousand miles away in Bath, everything that could be done in expectation of war was now in place. In common with the rest of the nation, the city authorities and the people of Bath paused and drew breath. They would not have long to wait.

At 11 a.m. the clock of peace finally stopped ticking. Shortly after 11, the Prime Minister broadcast to a waiting nation huddled around wireless sets that Britain and Germany were now at war. For the benefit of morning worshippers at Bath Abbey, a wireless set was placed in the pulpit to broadcast the Prime Minister's statement to a stunned congregation.

Following the Prime Minister's morning broadcast to the nation, the Chronicle *brought news of the outbreak of war to the citizens of Bath in a special edition on Sunday 3 September 1939.*

For the time being, on land, Hitler made no further moves in western Europe. For the British at home, the so-called 'Phoney War' began with a spate of air raid warnings, but no raiders came. And they were not to come for another nine months.

In Bath, life went on much as before, but with a new-found urgency. Evacuees from London and the south-east (including the staff of the Admiralty, moved to Bath from Whitehall) swelled the population of the city by many thousands. By October a National Register of all citizens in Britain had been completed and soon every Bath resident received a buff-coloured identity card that they had to carry with them at all times.

An example of the pragmatic approach to the demands of war adopted by residents of the city can be gleaned from a classified advertisement in the *Chronicle* of 4 September: '**Wanted** – Would kind person give or lend pram or push chair for mother with three small evacuated children under 5 years – 52 Dorset Street.'

CHAPTER 2

Changes in an Old City

The novelties of the black-out and the influx of thousands of war workers and evacuees to Bath were among the many changes to city life – hitherto unchanged for decades – that inspired an anonymous *Chronicle* journalist, known simply by his or her initials, 'P.S.', to pen this impression of a city coming to terms with its drastically altered circumstances. The article, entitled 'Changes in an Old City', appeared in the *Chronicle* of 8 November 1939:

War is one of the greatest scene-shifters in the world, for not only does it affect men and women, but the very country, towns and cities in which they live. Today the now scarcely noticed gas mask is carried by nearly everyone, and there is only momentary anxiousness as flights of aeroplanes drone overhead. The piles of sandbags outside important centres bring one back to the realities and the much-abused black-out acquaints one once more with the delights of the fireside and the stars on a clear night.

Bath like other large provincial centres that have received billetees and evacuees seems, to the careful observer, to be changing into a place sterner and stronger. To those familiar with London's busy streets and cosmopolitan character Bath seems to have caught a breath of that air. Bath is strangely full and busy. The city retains its dignity but an air of busy efficiency has been given to its bustling streets that has changed its character from a spa to a city conscious of its duties and obligations to the visitors.

As lunch-time approaches one notices, not now with surprise and a tinge of resentment, for the novelty has worn off, but with amazement at their numbers, the throngs of workers and the happy chatter of girls as they pour from the many extemporised offices that once housed famous people. The restaurants and cafes nearly all report good business; such business indeed, as has not been seen for many years, as the 'black-coated workers' teem into their open portals.

Bath has accepted with friendliness and sympathy its quota of workers and evacuees, sympathised with them for being separated from their dear ones, and extended to them the friendliness for which the 'Queen City of the West' has always been noted. But with the temporary cessation of meetings and activities of societies, the early closing of cinemas, theatres and dances, new clubs have sprung up almost overnight to bring good cheer into the hearts of Londoners. For war once again stirs the spirit of hospitality and new friendliness is bred, and old barriers are broken down.

Doors are opened in welcome and the visitors find new friends amongst sturdy 'Zomerset' folk. And if Bathonians air grievances connected with this sudden influx of visitors – for it is the Englishman's right to grumble – they realise after reflection that a bitter truth expressed in the Great War that 'in war there are no decencies' is only partly true, however bitter the experiences perhaps already undergone may be, for they can be forgotten.

The streets of Bath resound to new accents and if the cars are fewer in number, then one may walk in greater safety down its gracious streets. The queer twists of London 'cockney' mix incongruously with broad Bath and Somerset. Nearly all London's many accents may be heard in a short walk down the crowded pavements of Milsom Street or Southgate Street on a Saturday morning or evening.

It leads one to ponder on the possible effects of such a social revolution, but reflections are often broken as a party of men or girls pass by, speaking in a different accent and tone from that last group of pretty girls one encountered and smiled at only a few months ago. Shrill 'cockney' may resound along the streets but one feels that the owners of the voices will benefit in health from the clean country air and better conditions under which most of them now live, even if separated from home.

Little evacuees run excitedly along our streets and gaze in amazement or wonder at the city spread out below them from some distant height or famous view-point. 'Coo, isn't it lovely!' is the typical statement that is echoed and re-echoed by many a little stranger after he or she has climbed such a height. 'I have not met a friend of mine down here from London who doesn't like the place' is another such typical remark, this time from a billetee.

Rambles and walks in the city and on the clean, high hills have been organised, and on Sunday afternoons one may see the visitors energetically stepping out to some beauty spot and all will admit that the effort required to scale some height is well worth the while.

This mobile Citizen's Advice Bureau van is pictured in the Abbey Church Yard.

A street scene near Seven Dials car park, in which an air raid shelter had been built.
The Theatre Royal and Garrick's Head can be seen in the background. (Bath Reference Library)

Bath's new citizens speak well of the Queen City and the thoughtfulness with which its citizens have put up with the new conditions imposed upon them. There are wrongs to be considered and grievances to air, as is natural, for such a gigantic work cannot be accomplished without some trouble, but they will be adjusted in time.

Some of our streets may seem to lack the customary number of motor vehicles, but no-one can fail to notice the increase in cycles and horse-drawn traffic; cycle shops are doing a roaring trade in spite of that stiff upward trend in prices. What we may lose in speed we may make up in health. No keen cyclist grumbles at the rain or wind if adequately protected, but glories in it.

Only the hills of Bath present problems – but the run down them is a grand experience! Even on early closing days, when in pre-war days the city seemed almost empty, there are plenty of people to be seen about taking advantage of the comparative quietness to see Bath in greater comfort and detail.

Londoners are well used to houses steeped in literary, historical, or national associations, but as one of them expressed herself, 'some of us will soon become keen students of the history of Bath!' and this sums up adequately, one thinks, the feeling of many. The children are generally too young to appreciate perhaps, tradition and associations, but they love to play in and explore the twisting and narrow alley-ways and streets.

In spite of increasing prices, shops are doing a good trade. Those selling cycles, gramophones and wireless sets anticipate small booms. Indoor places of amusement are generally well attended, for a good show or a dance is a change from a fireside, however tempting the radio or thrilling the book.

By night, the streets of Bath, in common with towns and cities and villages all over the country, are comparatively deserted now. 'They can't black out

There may have been a war on, but love and romance continued to bloom. Mr John Pierce (an Army officer) and his bride Miss Sheila Blagrove were married at St Luke's, Wellsway, in February 1942. Among the guests are two members of the ATS – probably family.

the moon' is a popular song of the moment, but it seems to express what many people have seldom perhaps noticed before – the beauty of the stars and a moon riding in a crystal-clear sky. On dark, rainy nights the aspect is different and most people are indoors, but fine nights bring out the couples to enjoy the night air and their own company. From nearby heights Bath shows few lights now, and the moon and stars watch over the destiny of a Bath strangely changed, yet more interesting and fascinating and with infinitely more life.

Hitler was not going to spoil the day for these newly-weds. Mr G. Heddon and Miss B. Millard leave St Mark's, Lyncombe, in their suitably adorned bridal car.

CHAPTER 3

Life in Wartime Bath

With the outbreak of the Second World War the whole face of everyday life in the city of Bath was changed utterly. The influx of thousands of evacuees and war workers to the city put an untold strain on accommodation, people had to learn to live with the strict black-out regulations, petrol was rationed, and many aspects of normal life that were taken for granted during peacetime were swept aside as the whole nation geared up for war with Germany. Below are many of the principal changes to Bath life that marked its transition from a city at peace to a city at war.

EVACUEES

Bath was one of the designated reception areas for wartime evacuees from major British cities thought to be at risk from bombing attacks. At the outbreak of war the city received 7,000 children, some of the younger ones accompanied by their mothers, mainly from London. A further 13,000 were destined for the Bathavon and Keynsham areas. Popularly known as the 'vackees', those arriving in the city were billeted mainly with willing families who had been found and vetted by the authorities. Special trains with cheap fares were run occasionally to enable relatives and friends to visit the evacuees, but at Easter 1940 parents were advised not to take their evacuee children home for the holiday because of the risk of air raids. The process of evacuation itself and the splitting up of families was undoubtedly a traumatic experience for the majority of those concerned.

An evacuee baby is fitted with clothing by members of the WVS at Bath. Bags of clothing donated by Bath residents can be seen in the background. (Bath Reference Library)

In addition to the official evacuees, there were also the 'unofficial' evacuees, refugees and a huge tide of war workers into the city. This great influx of immigrants put a serious strain on accommodation in Bath and in October 1940 city councillors warned that 'saturation point' was not far off. In the same month it was reported that a party of sixteen people, bombed out of their homes in London, were occupying one flat in the city.

In March 1941 the *Chronicle* reported the story of a refugee French family who had found accommodation in the Kingsmead area of the city:

[They] had the good fortune to catch the last refugee boat leaving their country shortly after the capitulation of France, after a nightmarish journey from their home at Reims to St Jean de Luz by car when they were subject to dive bombing and machine gunning by Nazi aeroplanes.

Among others arriving in Bath from the blitzed capital were homeless babies aged between one and four, who were taken in by the Bombed Babies Home at Batheaston. Bath schools were also faced with accommodation problems. Early in 1941 a municipal day nursery was opened at Harington Place for evacuee mothers with young children, but it was forced to close two months later 'because of red tape'. By early 1943 the number of evacuees in the city had fallen from 7,000 to 224, but Bath remained an official reception area.

Typical of the semi-detached houses erected in Bath from the 1930s were those offered for sale on The Tyning estate. Type 'A' cost £900 with a garage; Type 'B' £695. To purchase one of these homes would have been beyond the means of many ordinary people: in 1939 a shorthand typist could hope to earn £125 per annum, a sergeant pilot in the RAF £226, and a surveyor £520.

CALL-UP

In common with every other town and city in Britain, Bath was subject to the National Service (Armed Forces) Act, which was passed by parliament on the first day of war. It made all men between the ages of eighteen and forty-one liable for conscription into the Armed Forces. A Schedule of Reserved Occupations was also published, which allowed deferment of call-up for key workers employed in one of the reserved occupations, for example skilled engineers at Stothert & Pitt engaged on war work.

In June 1939 Bath was able to report that conscientious objection was 'almost negligible'. However, the question of the 'excuse of conscience' was first discussed in the letters column of the *Chronicle* in March 1940 and the matter surfaced again from time to time in the early part of the war. The call-up of civilians continued to proceed at a measured pace as the following table records:

1940

February: 20–23s to register
May: Britain to call-up 2 million more men in age groups 19–36
June: the '28s (1912) to register. 300,000 expected from new call-up
December: Big call-up in next 4 months. Young men from reserved lists

1941

May: registration of girls in the 1919 and 1920 classes in Bath for ATS, WRENS, WLA etc.
August: the '44s. It was expected that about 600 Bath 44s – men born in 1897 – would register for war work. All men born in that year, unless they have already registered as ex-coal miners or ex-merchant seamen, or are exempted from registration by the National Service Acts, are instructed to attend at the Employment Exchange, James Street West.
September: the '19s. Over 300 Bath youths must register. Between 300 and 400 men born between 1 July and 31 December 1922 – the 18s and 19s – are expected to register for National Service in Bath.
December: Churchill announces expansion of recruitment. Men up to 50. Single women 20 to 30 years. Boys and girls 16 to 18 to register.
The 1910s to register. Women who were born in 1910 are reminded that they have to register for National Service unless they are exempted classes. Bath Employment Exchange officials estimate that between 600 and 700 local women of the 1910 class will sign on.

1942

August: 400 Bath girls in new call-up. The new call-up of women born in the first half of 1922 between 1 January and 30 June will affect about 400 women in Bath. Only single women or widows with no children will be taken. They will be drafted into the women's services, Land Army, or industry. Women born in 1899 are due next to register at the Employment Exchange.
September: Women of the 1898 age group to register at their local Employment Exchange for National Service. As the majority are married, they will be registered for part-time clerical and light factory work. About 600 will register at Bath. Classes called for registration for the first time are boys born between 1 March and 12 September 1926; girls born between 26 April and 12 September 1926.

1944

100 Bath boys and girls to register at local offices of the Ministry of Labour and National Service. The 17s and 18s – young men born between 1 April and 30 June 1926 – will be required to register under National Service Acts 1939–42. About 150 will register in Bath.

THE ADMIRALTY

With the outbreak of war, contingency plans drawn up to evacuate vital government departments from London were put into effect. On Sunday 17 September, the first of the Admiralty professional departments to be evacuated from Whitehall to Bath arrived in the city by special train. Many more were to follow at regular intervals over the coming months. However, many civil servants could not understand why they should be sent into the provinces while staff at the War Office, just across the road

Admiralty staff arrive in Bath on the outbreak of war in 1939. This is the scene outside the Empire Hotel.

in Whitehall, remained in London. Whatever the reasons for their evacuation to Bath, their arrival swelled the city's population by several thousand and when combined with the arrival of evacuees (as already described above), put a serious strain on Bath's ability to house them all. Admiralty staff were billeted with families across the city and in most instances the arrangements were satisfactory. However, the sum of one guinea given to billetors to cover a week's accommodation, bed and breakfast and evening meals became a matter of contention although it was never changed.

Most of the city's hotels were commandeered by the Admiralty for office accommodation, adding further to the city's inability to house both temporary and longer-term visitors. The Grand Pump Room Hotel in Stall Street was taken over by the Battleship Section of the Director of Naval Construction (DNC) where it remained until 1942, at which time it moved to the newly built Warminster Road hutments. DNC staff also occupied the Fernley Hotel at North Parade and St Paul's Church Rooms (now the Robin's cinema); the Finance Section took over a house in Vane Street and a Frigate Section at Widcombe Hall. When the Grand Pump Room Hotel was at risk from aerial attack in April 1942 the Pump Room itself was temporarily commandeered to provide office space while other sections moved up the Lansdown Road to the Royal School. The staff of the Engineer-in-Chief's Department had their offices at the Spa Hotel in North Road while the Naval Ordnance Department occupied the smaller Darlington Court nearby until they, too, moved to the Royal School. The Technical College in Beau Street was occupied by the Electrical Engineering Department, while the Pulteney Hotel in Pulteney Street (now Connaught Mansions) housed the Dockyard Department and later the Directorate of Contract Works and Supplies. Other Admiralty offices were at Oldfield School, Portland Place and the Museum in Queen Square. The Empire Hotel at Grand Parade was occupied by a number of Secretariat Branches and

the Staff of the Chief Inspector of Naval Ordnance also had offices there. Admiralty departments remained there for more than fifty years until they were removed to new premises at Abbey Wood, Filton. Kingswood School was used by Naval Accounts Department and by the Civil Engineer-in-Chief's Department, which also had part of the Royal School just down the hill.

BLACK-OUT

In these days of brightly lit shops and streets it is difficult to imagine life in the wartime black-out. During the summer of 1939, the public was given guidance on black-out restrictions so they could buy and prepare the necessary materials for their windows. On the evening of Friday 1 September 1939, three days before Britain declared war, the blackout proper began and from then on patrols of ARP wardens in tin hats and blue overalls patrolled the streets to make sure that from half an hour after sunset until half an hour before sunrise, no chinks of light from windows were visible that might guide in enemy bombers.

From AUSTINS to AUSTIN owners

THE BLACKOUT BRINGS IT HOME TO YOU . . . Creeping along the dark roads, taking an inevitable knock now and then from less careful drivers, your Austin is giving daily and night'y proofs of its sturdiness and reliability. It wouldn't be pleasant to find yourself stranded in some out of the way place in the bla.kout with so few garages and service stations a' out—and all of them closed—would it? Well, as your car is an Austin you won't be worrying.

. . . Aren't you GLAD you invested in an AUSTIN

To comply with black-out regulations, special black-out masks had to be fitted to the headlights of all motor vehicles.

Clock repairer Fred White of Milton Avenue was employed by Mallory's to maintain the city's public clocks, including the one on the Abbey tower, which is where he is standing here. (Bob White)

It was not long before the first cases for lighting offences were heard by the city magistrates. Fines were imposed on cyclists for having lights that did not comply with the Lighting Restrictions Order; on householders for 'causing a light to be displayed' in their homes; and on residents for flashing unscreened hand torches. Stern warnings were given about the importance of observing black-out regulations with threats that 'rigorous action' would be taken against offenders. It seems that no one could escape.

The use of compulsory car headlamp masks and the masking of traffic lights led to complaints from the public about safety. Black-out conditions undoubtedly made travelling difficult and the *Chronicle* warned its readers: 'It's that man again! When your train home is late, blame the blackout; and for the blackout, blame Hitler!' In February 1940 'Summer Time' was brought in early and retained all year round until 1941 when it was replaced with 'Double Summer Time'. The extra hour meant that clocks were two hours ahead of Greenwich Mean Time. Although this meant that it now got dark later in the evening, in the morning people had to make their way to work in twilight.

Needless to say, dozens of accidents were caused by the black-out. Many pedestrians suffered simple bumps and scrapes sustained from walking into trees in the dark or tripping off curbs, but in September 1939 the number of people killed in road accidents nationwide doubled. This figure did not include those who had fallen from trains at railway stations, crashed through glass roofs or inadvertently walked into rivers or canals. In Bath, incidents due to the black-out were plentiful and ranged from fatal accidents to minor bumps. A Twerton music teacher fell from a train when alighting onto what he thought was the platform; a fatal accident at Weston involving a pedestrian and a car driver led the court later on to rule that the driver was 'blameless'; and a man fell into Widcombe lock:

Bath Black-out Hero

Mr A.L.C. Wood of Blenheim Road, Newbridge Hill, Bath, has been awarded the Bronze Medal of the Royal Humane Society for his gallantry in plunging into a canal lock at Widcombe during the blackout and rescuing Mr Sidney Gledhill. Mr Wood is a partner in Widcombe Garages and when the call for help came, drove a car to the canal bank, switched the head lights to shine on the dark water and plunged in.

Happily, both Mr Gledhill and Mr Wood lived to see another day.

The blacking-out of public buildings such as the Assembly Rooms and the Guildhall presented problems that were not easily solved. Church services were also affected by the black-out. At the Abbey, service times had to be re-arranged: 'The morning services remain the same. The 3.15 Choral Evensong will be suspended. The 6.30 Choral Evensong with sermon will be put back to 3.30,' reported the *Chronicle*.

After D-Day, Bath's population along with the rest of Britain hoped that there would be a relaxation of the black-out. At the outbreak of war every bulb from the city's street lights had been removed and put into store. Early in September 1944 when staff from the City Engineer's Department unpacked the bulbs and tested each one to check its condition, they found to their dismay that most were unusable. Therefore fresh stocks had to be ordered in anticipation of the end of the black-out, which finally came on 17 September. The *Chronicle* reported on

The lights go on again. A scene at Grosvenor on 23 April 1945 when full street lighting was permitted for the first time since the outbreak of the war.

11 September that 'effort is being made to ensure that as many street lamps as possible will be lighted up in Bath on Sunday night – N-Night – switching over from "black-out" to "dim-out"'. However, it was not until April 1945 that the half-measure of 'dim-out' was turned up to 'full illumination' and the *Chronicle* was able to report with jubilation 'The lights of Bath go up again. For the first time since the war began, residents were able to "light up" without having to draw their blinds or curtains.' But the habits of six years of war were hard to break and many people kept their heavy black-out blinds and curtains for years to come.

TRANSPORT

Cars

In June 1939, three months before the outbreak of war, Whiting's Motor Works in Bath were offering a 1938 Flying Standard 12 Saloon de Luxe for £150. Not only was this price beyond the reach of the ordinary man in the street, but so also was the cost of running a car. Tramcar (later the bus) and train were still the principal means used by the majority of people for getting about. With the introduction of petrol rationing for private cars later that year, the volume of road traffic began to drop dramatically – from two million cars in 1939 to just 718,000 in 1943. On 2 October 1939 the *Chronicle*'s columnist 'Sul' described 'Our Car-less roads':

It is now possible to drive or walk about Bath without any personal risk (I mean in daylight), as the petrol rationing has almost cleared the streets of cars. In a long

The new range of Bedford trucks offered for sale by The Western Counties Automobile Co. Ltd at Argyle Street and Grove Street.

In spite of petrol rationing, taxi services were still available. This business card issued by 'Swift' Hire Services listed charges on the reverse side. Of special interest is the charge of 1s 3d for the first mile and 1s thereafter in the black-out. (Authors)

journey on Sunday, undertaken for business reasons, I only saw 15 cars and four lorries in 50 miles. Various observers, I notice, say that only one car in three was out on Sunday. My own impression is that the proportion was considerably less.

In view of the expected effect of the petrol rationing it seems strange that this particular moment should have been adopted to introduce the principle of unilateral waiting in Bath. Motorists have now no need to look for parks. There is plenty of room in the streets to stay a reasonable time. Most of the cars I noticed this morning were on official business and their drivers, consequently, have no petrol worries.

In January 1940 the fitting of compulsory masks for car lights came into force and it was later announced that because of possible confusion between air raid warnings and police car sirens, the latter would no longer be used. By mid-1942 there were about 3,900 private cars registered in Bath but some 650 licences were not renewed in the second quarter of that year. One reason for the decreased use of cars was the growing expense. Petrol was now much more expensive – in December 1939 it had risen to 1s 10d a gallon (the highest price since February 1924, when it was 1s 11d) – and it was only issued on proof of need. New taxation was imposed on private motorists, including a banded tax based on the horsepower rating of a vehicle, and as a result most motorists quickly conceded

defeat and put their cars into storage for the duration. At the end of August 1942 further restrictions were brought in to limit car usage and thereby save on fuel reserves. Private hire cars were banned from travelling between Bath and Bristol because of the newly imposed national statutory 10-mile limit.

Buses

In February 1940 an upheaval took place within the public transport system in Bath with the change-over from trams to buses, and it was estimated that the old tram rails soon to be ripped up for scrap would add £4,000 to the city's revenue. Early in 1942 more buses were promised for Bath shoppers. 'Important changes in the bus services in Bath come into effect as from Sunday next,' reported the *Chronicle* on 29 January. 'On most routes there will be increased services between certain daylight hours and reduced services in the evenings.' But in an attempt to regulate people's behaviour even more, the Ministry of Transport decreed in April that 'passengers must not try to board a vehicle out of turn and the order applies whether there is a queue sign or not'. Bath's new 'austerity buses' were noted by the *Chronicle* on 17 July 1942:

> They are buses with longitudinal seating which can accommodate 32 passengers seated and 24 standing – twice the number allowed in usual single-deckers. They are a wartime development and Bath has about a score operating on many routes.

Because of staff shortages and the fact that 'there's a war on', from February 1943 the Government imposed a travel curfew on Bath's bus services. Gloucester and Weston-super-Mare were similarly affected. Up until then the last buses on week nights left the city centre at 10 o'clock, but in February 1943 this was brought forward by half an hour. There was no change to the last buses on a Sunday evening, however. Early in 1944 the Regional Transport Commissioner gave his consent for certain slight modifications in one or two of Bath's bus services, but pointed out that they would not be put into operation unless more drivers and conductresses could be recruited. This situation remained virtually unchanged until the end of the war.

Rail

Britain's railways were heavily used by passengers and freight during the war. By 1943 passenger traffic had risen to nearly 70 per cent above its prewar level, an increase caused not only by petrol rationing but also because families dispersed across the country as a result of the war had to travel in order to see one another. Even so, trains were being cancelled at the rate between 1,000 and 1,500 services per week, not simply on account of enemy action, but also because of broken down and worn-out locomotives that were long overdue the breaker's yard.

The nationwide increase in rail traffic was mirrored in Bath; thanks to the city's convenient location on the national rail network, offering ease of access to London, the south coast and the Midlands, Bath's two railway stations were kept busy throughout the war years with passenger traffic ranging from Admiralty staff to evacuees and their families.

Bath had been served by two stations for the best part of one hundred years. The principal and older of the two, Bath Spa at Manvers Street, was served by the Great Western Railway on the mainline between Bristol and London. The other, at Green

Park and commonly known as 'the Midland', was served by two companies – the London, Midland & Scottish (LMS) and the Somerset & Dorset ('Slow & Dirty') – which ran to the Midlands and the south coast. During the blitz in 1942 the main passenger terminus building at Green Park was damaged by the blast from a bomb which destroyed the old S&D offices that stood opposite. The LMS goods station also suffered when the goods shed, offices, and eighteen coal trucks were burnt out.

During the August Bank Holiday weekend in 1942 the *Chronicle* observed that while passengers at Bath station were queueing up for seats to get away from the city, people from other places were 'arriving in crowds anxious to spend their Bank Holiday weekend in the city. Funny world!'

At Christmas 1942 the trains from Bath to London were crowded despite the familiar question on hoardings at railway stations everywhere asking 'Is your journey really necessary?'. 'Apparently Bath people thought it was', opined the *Chronicle*:

> More than this time last year bookings, mainly to London, have been much heavier. But it must be remembered that thousands of people who travelled by car a year ago have perforce to make their journeys this year on the iron road. As there are no special Christmas trains running and ordinary services have been much depleted many passengers are having to stand. Trains this morning were running well to schedule. Mail traffic is still heavy.

At Easter 1945, with the end of the war finally in sight, the *Chronicle* reported on 31 March:

> A large number of people have decided to spend what will probably be the last Easter of the war in Europe away from Bath, and there is a considerable rush on the railway. Many who are in Bath on essential work are going home for the holiday.

Peace came in little over a month, but the long struggle to return the railways to a semblance of normality was only just beginning.

WARTIME CHRISTMASES

The first Christmas of the war was celebrated in Bath in much the same way as those of previous years, although it did lack some of the glitter because of the strict black-out regulations then in force. Shop windows could not be lighted after dark but in an effort to capture something of the festive atmosphere, they were permitted early in the morning 'with a very pretty effect'.

Sensing a huge increase in the volume of mail in the run-up to the festive period, the Post Office drummed home to the public the importance of getting cards, letters and parcels off early with advertisements in the *Chronicle*: 'Christmas – Post Early. Wartime Christmas – Post EXTRA early!'. As the war progressed, the exhortation to post 'extra early' became applicable for much of the year as the Post Office was forced to reduce its deliveries and collections by more than half because of loss of staff to the armed forces. As early as Christmas 1939 Bath Post Office was already clearly suffering from the manpower shortage and advertised 'urgently required – able bodied men between the ages of 19 and 55 to assist with letter and parcel deliveries during the Christmas period. Rate of pay 1s 2½d per hour'.

As the effects of food rationing began to bite, the *Chronicle* published all kinds of useful tips on how to cater for the family at Christmas. An invitation to

Christmas greetings from the Chronicle *in 1941: 'Joy Riding Without Petrol'.*

attend cookery demonstrations in the Electricity Showroom at the Old Bridge appeared in the *Chronicle* early in December 1939, offering to show housewives 'how to make Christmas cakes from wartime recipes'.

> Price of turkeys are [sic] controlled. They soared too high – so Lord Woolton stepped in. The price of turkeys is controlled as of today. This decision came as a great surprise to retailers in Bath and the rest of the country. They complain that having to buy in a competitive market they now stand to lose heavily.

On 14 December 1940 the *Chronicle* offered advice about catering for Christmas parties:

Sandwiches for Christmas Parties
Novel Ideas for Easy Wartime Entertaining

Sandwiches will be the mainstay of many informal wartime Christmas parties. Given the variety of new fillings and careful cutting, they can be the most appetising as well as the most practical fare for the present time. For parties let them be small and slim, and cut in different shapes. Instead of keeping to the conventional fillings, many of which are subject to rationing difficulties, go out for a touch of novelty. Use brown as well as white bread for your party sandwich, and ring other changes by making fingers of toast or plain biscuits as the foundation of some of them. Remember, too, that now that cakes are plainer, both adults and children like sweet sandwiches so let yours be sweet as well as savoury. Here are four new suggestions for sandwich spreads all made with wartime

ingredients and planned by the Stork Margarine Cookery Service. Cheese or chutney spread, sardine cream, banana and marmalade, almonds and raisins.

Shortages of meat also caused problems in catering for the traditional Christmas dinner:

Your Christmas Dinner
Why Meat is Scarce This Week
This is due to several causes. There are of course our losses of cargo boats to be considered. For another thing there are the demands of the fighting services to be met, not only at home but in the Middle East and elsewhere. Then again, the outbreaks of Foot and Mouth Disease in various parts of the country have meant the slaughter and incineration of considerable numbers of animals which otherwise would have been available for food. This applies especially to pork which is practically unobtainable.

For those unfortunate enough to be spending the season of goodwill in a hospital bed, it was 'Christmas as usual'. On Christmas Eve the nurses of the Royal United went on carolling tours of the wards and at noon on Christmas Day all patients who were not 'on diet' were invited to tuck in to the seasonal fare provided. On Boxing Day afternoon the Mayor of Bath made a round of visits at the city's hospitals where he helped Santa Claus to hand out presents to the children. Through Bath's six wartime Christmases the *Chronicle* reported there was always 'plenty to eat and plenty of fun' with 'special efforts for the kiddies'.

Just before Christmas 1943 it was announced that there was a possibility of oranges being available before the festive season got underway:

These, if not specially reserved for children, are available for sale on production of ration books. Many suppliers find that people come in from the surrounding country, even from Bristol, and as retailers cannot refuse to sell so long as ration books are shown, it sometimes happens that they have no supplies left when their regular customers arrive later.

For those who missed out on oranges at Christmas 1943 there would be a long wait, over a year until early 1944, when came the fruitful news that there would be 'oranges for all at Bath':

Everybody in Bath should get 1lb of oranges towards the end of next week. It is a general distribution and the arrival of the oranges in the shops will depend on transport. The oranges, which are said to be Valencios, are the first from Spain since the war. Supplies may allow 1lb each per ration book and retailers are required to mark the ration book for the reservation period, which lasts for five days.

With the war over in 1945 but with food rationing still in force, the celebration of a traditional Christmas in prewar style was still some way off.

CLUBS AND HOSTELS FOR THE ARMED FORCES

Food catering and accommodation for members of HM Armed Forces visiting the city on leave were provided by the YMCA in Broad Street, the Red Shield

Club Hostel in Northgate Street, TOC H in Grove Street, and the Women's Services Club run by Bath Soroptimists in Walcot Street. In October 1942 a US Red Cross Club was opened at the Lansdown Grove Hotel to provide a 'snatch of home' for American servicemen on leave in the city. Some American servicemen who were prepared to 'pay the extra money for a few comforts of the home', stayed instead at hotels and bed and breakfasts in the city. However, accusations of overcharging the 'Doughboys' by managers and proprietors found their way into the pages of the *Chronicle*:

Bath Catering Ramp Complaint
Prices that Hurt American Soldiers' Pride

American soldiers spending their leaves in Bath are complaining that they are being defrauded by a small minority of Bath's hotel keepers and cafe proprietors who, they allege, demand extravagant prices.

When a member of the American forces gets a leave he is allotted a certain town and is officially supposed to stay at the local Red Cross Club. If he visits Bath he is recommended to the American Red Cross Club in Lansdown Grove where accommodation is available.

I am told by an American official that often the club is filled to capacity, and then through the courtesy of the English organisations such as the YMCA, Salvation Army and TOC H, every effort is made to provide accommodation for an American soldier somewhere else.

While wishing to be scrupulously fair to the Red Cross authorities one US soldier said that when they are on leave some of them like a little more luxurious accommodation, and they feel that at a hotel they can enjoy a few comforts of the home which they lack in camp.

My Allied friend said that in the States, where the standard of living is much higher, one has to pay 25*s* for bed and breakfast at an hotel, but he did not think those charges should be charged in this country where the standard of living is not so high. 'It hurts the boys' pride to know they are being overcharged, but they pay the extra money for a few comforts of the home,' he said.

In Bath, if our Allies want a 'few comforts of the home' they must pay, at some hotels 16*s* 6*d* and 18*s* 6*d* for bed and breakfast only, for one night. Before the war the usual price for bed and breakfast at a good class hotel was 10*s* 6*d*. I am told that a reasonable wartime fee today is 12*s* 6*d* in Bath. Prices charged at local boarding houses are 8*s* 6*d* for bed and breakfast. At a few establishments I am glad to note a charge of only 5*s* is made for members of the Forces. In Trowbridge this week it was stated that an American soldier was asked to pay 29*s* 6*d* for bed and breakfast.

The ramp also operates at restaurants. At one cafe, an American told me, the manager said: 'I always charge more to the US soldiers because they have the money.' The American was charged 5*s* for an ordinary meal. I am officially informed that Food Control Committees have control over prices charged for meals but no control over prices charged for accommodation.

Can something be done to stop this ramp, which is being operated by a few people to exploit American soldiers who spend their leaves in Bath? If not, the Queen City of the West may have a stigma on its name when the Doughboys are way back home again.

ROYALTY IN BATH

Bath enjoyed the patronage of several Royals during the Second World War. The King and Queen visited the city in the wake of the blitz in April 1942 to inspect the damage and express their solidarity with the citizens of Bath, but the most frequent Royal visitor was Queen Mary. During the war she lived at Badminton House, the country seat of the Duke of Beaufort. Her visits, mostly shopping expeditions, began in 1939, as revealed by this front-page report from the *Chronicle* on 11 December:

Queen Mary Does Her Christmas Shopping in Bath
Drama of Surprise Call at Woolworth's, Visits to Colmer's and Jolly's
Queen Mary spent two hours Christmas shopping in Bath this morning. She visited Woolworth's, Stall Street, Colmer's in Union Street, and Jolly's in Milsom Street, the famous shopping thoroughfare of the West of England. The visit was a thrill for both shop assistants and the general public, for it was quite unexpected.

Monday mornings are generally very quiet in most of the business houses in the city, and often time is utilised by the assistants in tidying up after the Saturday rush and making preparations for business later in the day. One can judge, therefore, the surprise of Mr T. Kirkpatrick, manager of the Bath branch of Messrs F.W. Woolworth & Co, when a breathless assistant rushed into his office and told him that Queen Mary was on the premises. He at once went to the Royal visitor and escorted her around.

Queen Mary, a frequent wartime visitor to Bath, is seen here in 1941 at Denewood Grange, the special home for 'bombed babies' at Batheaston.

Attended by the Duchess of Beaufort, her niece, and Lady Cynthia Colville, Queen Mary first made a tour of the basement where there were already a large number of shoppers. Her purchases included some table games, six packs of cards, toys, Christmas cards, Christmas decorations, handkerchiefs, jewellery, fancy drapery, pictures and boxes of cottons. They numbered in all well over 50 articles. Outside in Stall street there was a big crowd assembled to get a glimpse of Her Majesty as she left.

Sometimes Queen Mary was accompanied by other members of the Royal family on her visits to the city, including the Princess Royal and the Duchess of Kent – and on one occasion, in May 1941, by the writer Osbert Sitwell. Among the department stores she patronised were Evans & Owen in Bartlett Street, Williams' and Jolly's, both in Milsom Street, and Colmer's in Union Street. She was fond of antiques and one of the Bath shops she visited was Angell's in Milsom Street. In December 1943 she paid a visit to the George Gregory bookshop in Green Street to buy a book as a Christmas gift for the King. It was Williamson and Howett's *Oriental Field Sports*, lavishly bound in two volumes, published in 1819. In the following year she visited an exhibition of Chinese art at the Victoria Art Gallery in Bridge Street. The projected postwar 'Plan for Bath', conceived by Sir Patrick Abercrombie, also interested her, and she visited a special exhibition about it in February 1945.

Another royal visitor to Bath was the Emperor Haile Selassie I, King of Kings, Lion of Judah, the ruler of Ethiopia, following the seizure of his country by the Italians in 1936. He came to Bath as a refugee with his family and servants to live at Fairfield House, Newbridge Road. In May 1941 the Emperor was able to return to Addis Ababa and the Empress gave a reception at Bath to celebrate his re-entry into the capital. There were sixty guests, including the Mayor of Bath, who proposed a toast to the Emperor and expressed the city's delight at his return home.

In September 1943 the 'Ethiopian Prince and Princess' left Fairfield House, but the Emperor's eldest daughter, Princess Tenaagne Worq, stayed until she could join her parents with her two sons, aged fourteen and thirteen, her youngest brother Prince Sahle, and the remainder of her staff. Following the departure of the last members of the family, the house, with the exception of the caretaker, stood empty for over ten years.

The elder of the present writers remembers attending a children's Christmas party at Fairfield House. The invitation came as a result of his being a classmate of one of the Emperor's grandsons at a Bath kindergarten.

CHAPTER 4

If the Enemy Should Come

DEFENCE ON THE GROUND

The Home Guard

During peacetime, Bath was home to four Territorial Army units who shared a common headquarters at the Drill Hall on the Lower Bristol Road. They were the North Somerset Yeomanry, the 129th (South Wessex) Infantry Brigade, the 43rd (Wessex) Division Royal Engineers, and the 4th Battalion the Somerset Light Infantry. When war was declared in September 1939 these territorial units were mobilised and sent off to war.

For many Bath citizens, the presence of the newly formed Home Guard was the only obvious sign of the city's military defence provisions. On 14 May 1940 men who were British subjects, aged between seventeen and sixty-five, and not engaged in military service (most because of their age or health) were urged via a broadcast by Anthony Eden, Secretary of State for War, to volunteer for the Local Defence Volunteers (LDV) , later called the Home Guard. This plea came at the height of the invasion fever that swept the country, prompting the nation to muster all means at its disposal to repel German invaders should they come.

'Dad's Army': members of the Fairfield Park Company, 5th Somerset (Bath City) Battalion, Home Guard. (Gordon Banks)

All ranks of the Bath Home Guard's 5th Battalion enjoy a dinner together at Christmastide.

The unpaid volunteer part-time soldiers of the LDV came from all walks of life and their task was to support the Army. This included guarding vital installations such as gas works, railways, roads and bridges. Within two days of Eden's broadcast, the *Chronicle* reported that over 600 men in Bath had enrolled for a 'Home Defence Corps as parashooters [sic]'.

The Bath garrison came into being on 22 May 1940 and at first was known as the Bath Company of the LDV. By August it had been raised to battalion strength and now comprised two Home Guard battalions – the 5th Somerset (Bath City) and the 6th Somerset (Bath Admiralty). Throughout their four-year existence, relations between the two battalions were cordial and a number of combined exercises took place. When they were finally stood-down in November 1944 the battalion strengths were as follows: 5th (Bath City) Battalion – 1,765 officers and men, 143 women auxiliaries; 6th (Bath Admiralty) Battalion – 960 officers and men, 77 women auxiliaries.

Short on uniforms, rifles and ammunition, but with boundless enthusiasm, Bath's Home Guard had to make do initially with 'Home Guard' armbands in place of uniforms, and with a motley collection of broom handles and pitchforks as weapons. As far as the latter is concerned, the balance was redressed in October 1940 when a consignment of 1,100 American rifles was issued to the city's two battalions.

Although named the 5th Somerset (Bath City) Battalion, the formation included in its catchment area Bathampton, Batheaston, Bathford, Charmy Down, Claverton, Dunkerton, Freshford, Limpley Stoke, Newton St Loe, North and South Stoke, Swainswick and Wellow. Battalion headquarters were at 15 Queen Square, where Lieutenant-Colonel G.H. Rogers was the commanding officer.

Members of the City Engineer's section of the ARP leave Victoria Park en route to a parade in 1941. (H. Hamlen)

The 6th Somerset (Bath Admiralty) Battalion was commanded by Lieutenant-Colonel W.C. Brown (Head of Common Services at the Admiralty), and was made up from Admiralty personnel in Bath, including many naval officers. Its headquarters were at 6 Edward Street. Although primarily concerned with the protection of Admiralty sites in the city, the 6th Battalion also patrolled the city streets at night alongside men of the 5th Somerset (Bath City) Battalion. In the build-up to D-Day men of the 6th Battalion guarded the railway tunnel at Bath when the ammunition trains were passing through on their way to the south coast.

Men of both battalions played an important role in the Bath blitz and received awards for bravery, notably members of the 6th Battalion who rescued guests trapped in the ruins of the Regina Hotel after it received a direct hit. Company Sergeant Major James Leslie of the 6th Battalion was awarded the George Medal. After the blitz the main priority was to get the city back to work and once more both battalions were actively engaged in the repair of damaged buildings and industrial premises, salvaging and storing furniture from bomb damaged premises, anti-looting patrols and traffic control.

Prior to the *Baedeker* blitz of 1942 (see Chapter 5), the city was without anti-aircraft defences, but soon afterwards the 6th Battalion was equipped with twelve 2-inch rocket projectors and eight 40-mm Bofors guns. In addition to these weapons, five German flak guns were obtained from naval sources for the defence of the city. Unfortunately for Bath, however, these defence measures came a little too late; the damage had been done and the Germans did not bomb the city again.

Civil Defence Services – ARP and Supporting Services

Air Raid Precaution (ARP) services covered a variety of responsibilities including the provision of wardens, mostly part-timers, whose principle job was to report on the fall of bombs, fires and casualties to the Bath City ARP Control Centre. At the beginning of the war this was located at 2 Broad Street, but in 1941 the centre was moved out to Apsley House at Newbridge Hill to the west of the city, with a back-up centre at the Forester's Arms public house at Foxhill.

Shortly after war was declared a big rumpus blew up between city councillors and the newly formed Emergency Committee, whose job it was to manage Bath's air raid precautions. The committee stood accused by some councillors of extravagance, wasting money, and favouritism when it came to employing full-time ARP staff. The row spilled over into the pages of the *Chronicle*, whose report of 3 October 1939 makes amusing reading:

Dictatorship Charges over ARP Wage Bill

There were stormy scenes in the Bath Council Chamber this morning over the 'dictatorial' powers of the Emergency Three (the Mayor, Major G.D. Lock, and Mr Walter Barrett) and the huge wages bill incurred for ARP.

The 'Big Three' were attacked with a vigour rarely heard in the Council and the Mayor defended the Emergency Committee with as much energy. He hotly resented being pilloried in this way, declaring that if bombs fell and everything humanly possible had not been done to safeguard the lives of civilians, the Committee would have been accused of 'homicide'.

Mr L.N. Punter lamented that financial control had passed out of the hands of the Council, but the Mayor, answering the declaration that the 'wages' bill is more than £2,000 a week, retorted that the share Bath must pay is only £225 a week, together with a 'trivial expenditure' on the rent of buildings. Mr J. Plowman, Chairman of the Finance Committee, urged that £250 a week could be saved on ARP wages and demanded a cut in the fire service.

Ald Hunt: 'We are fighting a war to get rid of one dictator but we have put three in his place. We have got our Mussolini, Hitler and Stalin.'

Ald Bateman: 'Which is which?'. (Laughter.)

Mr G.W. Barrow, Charge Officer at St John's (Bathwick) Depot Casualty Service, and Mr R.C. Chapman, a Party Leader, pictured in October 1941.

When Captain Hopkins stepped down as Mayor of Bath in November 1939, he made a valedictory speech during which he criticised the 'ARP baiters' as he called them. He denied any extravagance and contrasted the £40,000 spent on ARP with the £65,000 spent on the City of Bath Boys' School and the £47,000 spent on the Girls' School. 'Our inhabitants are safe so long as they are educated', he cynically observed.

Accusations of extravagance rumbled on for a few months more, but eventually the bickering died away when both the Council and the Emergency Committee realised they had to get on with the serious business of making sure

'Put that light out!': volunteers from East Twerton (St Peter's Post) of 'E' Group Wardens in December 1942. Colonel Newnham (Head Warden) is in the centre of the front row. (A.C. Urch)

Bath was prepared for enemy air attacks should they come. If the Council had got its way over cuts to ARP and fire services, Bath would have been even more ill-prepared for the heavy raids that came two and a half years later.

In terms of organisation, ARP in Bath comprised a wide variety of specialised services. These were as follows:

Rescue Services. Their task was to rescue people who were trapped in bomb damaged buildings, to remove the dead and to make safe damaged buildings.

First Aid. Incident doctors were on call and might be called to the scene of an incident to render life-saving medical treatment to casualties, whether trapped or suffering from shock.

First Aid Parties. Stretcher bearers and ambulance drivers, whose job was to bring the injured to hospital at St Martin's, Combe Down, and the Royal United, Combe Park, or to Casualty Collecting Posts (CCPs). There were twenty-two CCPs in the city itself and a further twenty-nine in the surrounding district of Bathavon, which extended from the Viaduct Hotel at Limpley Stoke to the vicarage at Newton St Loe, and from Charmy Down airfield to Midford village.

Decontamination Service. Working in protective oilskin clothing, their unenviable task was to decontaminate buildings, roads and vehicles, etc., from persistent gases (i.e. those that would cover objects on exploding, rather than being carried in the air as a non-persistent gas). The main cleansing agent they used was bleach powder.

Gas Identification Service. Its specialist officers were to visit the scene of an incident to confirm the type of gases used (although, thankfully, poison gas never was used against Britain during the Second World War).

Roof Spotters, Fire Watchers and Fire Guards. Their job was to help the fire service by noting where incendiaries fell and dealing with them before they got out of control.

The Fire Services. In September 1939 trained part-time firefighters of the Auxiliary Fire Service (AFS) in Bath were called up for full-time service to work alongside the existing full-time firefighters, whose headquarters were at Bath City Fire Station at Cleveland Bridge. In August 1941 the National Fire Service (NFS) was formed to take control of the local authority-run fire brigades for the duration of the war.

The Police. In addition to their principal role of maintaining law and order in the city, the Bath police also worked with the ARP wardens patrolling the streets. They sounded the air raid sirens, visited public shelters that were on their beats, and were involved in crowd and traffic control following a raid incident. Bath Police Headquarters were at the Central Police Station in Orange Grove.

Volunteers for fire watching duties line up to register at Bath Employment Exchange early in the war.

Before they were assigned to firefighting parties, volunteers had to undergo two stages of training. This card certifies that Mrs Falconer (aged forty-seven) of Bath was a member of a firefighting party and that she underwent training on 31 August 1942. (Authors)

CITY OF BATH.

CIVIL DEFENCE.

Nᵒ 1073

This is to Certify that

Folio No.

Trained—Stage I.

Stage II.

Block No.

is a member of a Fire-fighting party organised by the Bath City Council and possesses the powers of entry and of taking steps for extinguishing fire or for protecting persons or property from fire, which are conferred by the Fire Precautions (Access to Premises) (No. 2) Order, 1941.

Authorising Officer.

Town Clerk.

Date

The Observer Corps. Under the operational control of the Air Ministry, members of the Observer Corps were skilled in the art of aircraft identification and acted as the first line of warning of enemy air attack. From three vantage points in the city, including one at Lansdown, they maintained a constant look-out for enemy aircraft, reporting the numbers, type, height, and direction of flight to RAF Fighter Command, the Army's Ack-Ack Command and the air raid warning authorities, who would then scramble fighters and alert anti-aircraft gun batteries and civil defence commanders.

Women's Voluntary Service. From their headquarters at 8 Quiet Street, members of the WVS helped with placing evacuees with families in the city and also attempted to find empty houses for large families and other people from bombed areas coming daily to Bath. The WVS also staffed the Food Control Office and helped at the city's hospitals.

DEFENCE IN THE AIR

The Royal Air Force

For the citizens of wartime Bath, aircraft buzzing overhead from the two RAF fighter airfields nearby were a familiar and reassuring occurrence. To the Observer Corps spotters in their bunkers and eager little boys in school playgrounds, the difference between a Spitfire and a Beaufighter would have been instantly recognisable; because of the different engine noises they could tell them apart even with their eyes closed. The skies over Bath reverberated to the sounds of an exciting variety of powerful and heavily armed RAF fighter aircraft, ranging from single-engined Spitfires and Hurricanes, Defiants and Typhoons, to the heavier twin-engined Blenheims and Beaufighters, Whirlwinds and Mosquitoes.

RAF Colerne. In 1940, on a wide expanse of pasture beside the Old Fosse Way 4 miles north-east of the city, the RAF built an airfield and called it Colerne after the neighbouring village. Some 2,000 years earlier a Roman nobleman had lived in style on this very spot with his family, servants and slaves in his fine country villa. Although designed and constructed as a maintenance unit for the storage and assembly of military aircraft, the newly built RAF Colerne was taken over by Fighter Command in September 1940. Like many other RAF stations the length and breadth of Britain in wartime, Colerne played host to its share of airmen from the far corners of the British Empire who had rallied to the call to arms. Canadians, Australians, New Zealanders, Rhodesians and South Africans – not forgetting those from the British Isles – found themselves posted to Colerne.

Between 1940 and 1945 Colerne accommodated a succession of thirty-two fighter squadrons that protected Bath, Bristol and south-west England from marauding German bombers. Later in the war some of its Mosquito squadrons flew daring intruder sorties deep into enemy occupied Europe to seek out and destroy German aircraft on their own airfields. Top secret installation work was also carried out at Colerne during 1942 by RAF maintenance staff, fitting the latest radar equipment into nightfighter aircraft.

In the early hours of 19 November 1942 a Pathfinder Halifax bomber in distress crash-landed at Colerne. It had been set on fire as it neared the Alps, returning

Boulton Paul Defiant fighter aircraft, similar to this example, were based at Colerne and Charmy Down airfields during 1941. (Authors)

De Havilland Mosquito nightfighter aircraft, similar to this NF Mk II, operated from Colerne in 1942. (Authors)

from a raid on Turin, and the pilot had nursed his badly damaged aircraft home across Switzerland and France to a successful emergency landing at Colerne.

But imagine the disbelief on the faces of Colerne's fire and ambulance crews when they discovered that the seven-man aircraft was empty except for the pilot, Squadron Leader Basil Robinson, who emerged from the wrecked bomber with little more than a scratch. Robinson had ordered his crew to bale out over Italy when it looked as though the fire was burning out of control. Amazingly, just before he was about to follow his crew and 'hit the silk', the fire died out and he decided to risk it and try to reach home singlehandedly, which he did 800 miles later.

During the Bath blitz in April 1942 the two RAF nightfighter squadrons based at Colerne (125 Squadron) and Charmy Down (87 Squadron) scrambled their Hurricanes and Defiant fighters, but managed to shoot down only one of the

German raiders. Shortly after D-Day, a wing of three Mosquito nightfighter squadrons arrived at Colerne and roamed nightly over France searching for targets of opportunity, with considerable success. In January 1945 Colerne achieved a place in aviation history when it became the RAF's first permanent jet fighter base, albeit for less than a month, as 616 Squadron worked up to strength on the Gloster Meteor III.

RAF Charmy Down. Three miles to the south-west across the deep green gouge of the St Catherine's valley that plunges dramatically away between Colerne and the A46 north towards Stroud, a satellite airfield for Colerne was built on the hilltop at Charmy Down. At 690 ft above sea-level it was one of the highest airfields in the British Isles. Nine squadrons flew operationally from this windswept field at various times from November 1940 until the last operational squadron flew away in February 1943 and Charmy Down was turned over to training RAF aircrew. Men and machines of the US 9th Air Force were temporary occupants during the spring and summer of 1944 in the build-up to D-Day, but left soon after and the airfield was returned to use by the RAF.

Two RAF squadrons engaged in top secret night interception trials operated from Charmy Down during 1942. A small number of Douglas Havoc twin-engined fighters were fitted with a powerful 'Turbinlite' spotlight with which to illuminate enemy bombers at night. If an enemy aircraft got caught in the glare of the spotlight, a Hurricane fighter flying close to the Turbinlite Havoc would close in and shoot the bomber down. This Heath-Robinson affair was beset with problems from the word go and the Turbinlite experiment was eventually abandoned in early 1943.

THE AMERICANS

Unlike many towns and villages in southern England during the massive build-up to D-Day in June 1944, Bath did not have any American troops billeted in the city, although many did visit when on leave.

However, airmen of the US IXth Tactical Air Command with the 425th Night Fighter Squadron and Air Force Service Command Units were stationed temporarily at Charmy Down, which was called 'AAF Station No. 487'.

In 1940 work began on building a large military hospital adjacent to the Royal United Hospital at Combe Park. Originally intended for use by British forces, the completed buildings were taken over by the US Army in August 1942 and then became known as the 152nd Station Hospital. Sick and wounded military personnel located within a radius of approximately 50 miles of Bath were cared for and treated at the hospital, which had 14 wards and 394 beds. It offered a range of patient care that included acute surgical, general medicine, orthopaedics, respiratory, neuropsychiatric and ENT facilities. The Americans remained at Combe Park until after the war had ended, returning home in late 1945. At this time the now vacant hospital facilities were turned over to the Ministry of Health and became known as the Manor Hospital (today called the Royal United Hospital North).

Troops of the US 1st Army, commanded by General Omar N. Bradley and with headquarters in Bristol, were billeted across the west of England, from Cornwall to Gloucestershire, and in towns and villages around Bath including High Littleton, Blagdon, Wickwar, Chipping Sodbury, Trowbridge and Beckington.

CHAPTER 5

Blitz on Bath

A DISASTER WAITING TO HAPPEN

The morning of Saturday 25 April 1942 in wartime Bath had dawned sunny and bright, an ordinary spring day with the promise of a clear night to come. Citizens went about their business and tried not to think too hard about the war that had been going on for two and a half years. Later that day, as Bathonians were tucking into their teas in the late afternoon, several hundred miles away at airfields in enemy occupied France, German bomber crews gathered to receive their operational briefings for the coming night's raid over England.

A number of bombs had fallen within the city boundaries during the first two years of war, but all were strays and intended for targets elsewhere. Even so, fatalities had occurred: on 16 March 1941 three men and three children were killed at Twerton, and on 11 April 1941 eleven people lost their lives when buildings were destroyed in the Dolemeads area of Widcombe. Both incidents had taken place during heavy raids on Bristol. But the bombs that were soon to fall on Bath were not meant for anywhere else.

Hitler had called for maximum effort from his bomber units in the West to avenge the RAF's recent fire raids on the ancient Baltic ports of Rostock and Lübeck. Only three days before the raids on Bath, Exeter had been bombed in the first of the *Baedeker* raids, so called after a comment made on 27 April 1942 by the German Foreign Office about the Luftwaffe henceforth bombing every city marked with three stars in the famous German *Baedeker* tour guides.

A Dornier Do 217E-4 of Kampfgeschwader *40. Bomber aircraft of this type took part in the* Baedeker *raids on Bath in 1942.* (Authors)

Firefighters at work in the James Street West area during the blitz.

From the beginning of the war, Bath's Civil Defence organisation had carried out elaborate rehearsals from time to time in preparation for possible air attacks against the city. But when the time came they were unprepared and the raids quite unexpected – Bath was not considered to be a prime target for German bombers. For the same reason the city was unprotected by ack-ack guns or barrage balloons, and the airborne interception radar sets as fitted to British nightfighter aircraft of the period were fairly new and underdeveloped. Thus, undefended and with clear skies above, the citizens of Bath unwittingly became victims of a disaster that was waiting to happen.

At about 9.30 on the evening of 25 April, as Bath cinema-goers headed for home in the black-out, some eighty German bombers took to the air from bases in France, laden with deadly cargoes of high explosive and incendiary bombs – their target, Bath. The first aircraft made landfall over the Dorset coast at 10.25 p.m. and headed north towards their objective. Pathfinder flares to illuminate Bath for the incoming bombers went down shortly before 11.20 p.m. and as the first high explosive and incendiary bombs whistled down onto the unprotected city, the air raid sirens began to wail. In the clear moonlight conditions the Junkers Ju 88 and Dornier Do 217 bombers, supported by a handful of the older He 111s and Do 17s, were able to swoop very low to drop their bombs with considerable accuracy. The first stick fell between Crescent Gardens and the Gas Works on the Upper Bristol Road, where a gas holder was destroyed.

Thousands of incendiary bombs and many tons of high explosives burned and blasted the city as wave after wave of low-flying bombers ranged overhead unopposed. Civil Defence workers, ambulance crews and firefighters toiling to

Devastation caused by a high explosive bomb in the Upper Bristol Road near the bottom of Marlborough Lane.

save their city were raked with machine-gun fire as the bombers swooped down over the burning streets. The all-clear sounded at 12.11 a.m., with another alarm sounding at 12.46 a.m., but the final all-clear went at 1.10 a.m. A few brave souls ventured out of their shelters to take a look at the damage and breathed a sigh of relief that the raid was finally over, but more was to come and soon.

It is clear that the Germans had singled out Bath for special treatment that night. As soon as the bombers had returned to their bases they were refuelled and re-armed and sent straight back to the stricken city, taking off at 3.30 a.m. By this time Bath was well ablaze and it was an easy task for the Junkers and Dornier bomber crews to find the city again and stoke the fires with dozens more bombs. After a lull that had lasted a little over three hours, at 4.35 a.m. on Sunday morning the sirens wailed again and people took to the shelters for the second time that night. An estimated forty enemy aircraft reappeared and began to pound the city mercilessly. Because it was known that a large number of fires had been started in Bath during the first phase of the operation, the further use of incendiaries was not considered necessary, so consequently high explosives were used almost exclusively in this raid. Hurricane and Beaufighter nightfighters flew standing patrols between 4 a.m. and 7.30 a.m., but failed to shoot down any of the raiders. With the first light of day, like a horde of vampires, the raiders shrank away and the full extent of the devastation across the city became apparent.

In the first phase of the raid most of the damage had been concentrated in the Kingsmead and Upper Bristol Road areas, while in the second phase considerable

destruction was wrought on residential property, especially in the Twerton, Lower Bristol Road and Oldfield Park areas. Some seven factories were seriously damaged including Stothert & Pitt's Newark and Victoria Works and the Horstmann Gear Company's Albion Works. Many buildings were still burning the morning after, but the NFS had managed to contain most of the fires. Some streets were totally destroyed while others were obstructed with debris that hampered the work of rescue teams searching for the dead and injured still trapped inside collapsed buildings. The brave efforts of Bath's Civil Defence workers and the NFS were augmented by teams from Bristol, Keynsham, Devizes, Swindon and Weston-super-Mare, and from as far afield as Cheltenham, Gloucester and even Coventry. All day long rescue teams worked to release survivors, while others made safe the buildings damaged by bombs and tried to restore some semblance of order to the stricken city. Members of the WVS manned mobile kitchens bringing much needed hot food and drinks to exhausted rescue workers and to those families unlucky enough to have been 'bombed out'.

Medical and surgical teams had been alerted to receive casualties at the city's two main hospitals, the Royal United and St Martin's. Consulting surgeon at St Martin's, Dr F. Kohn – who had fled to England before war broke out in 1939 as a refugee from his native Czechoslovakia – recalled the ordeal at the hospital during the two nights of bombing:

Casualties had been arriving, all of them brought to Ward 1, which we had designated as a reception ward. There they were sorted out according to the

Members of the Home Guard in discussion against a background of bomb debris in Kingsmead Street.

In New King Street on the Sunday morning, the Home Guard keep watch near the ruins of a house demolished by a high explosive bomb, while in the background a family surveys a bomb crater in the road. The smoke is from buildings still burning on the opposite side of the street.

severity of their injuries and the degree of shock from which they were suffering. After my experience during the many raids on London, I knew how dangerous it could be to start with too much activity at once. We therefore gave only first aid at the beginning, initiated shock treatment, cleaned the patients and gave them pain-killing drugs. As long as the raid lasted no operative activity was carried out. Then, just as we were going to begin operating, the second wave of raiders came in and started bombing again. We got ready to receive more casualties, and they came! St Martin's admitted during these two nights over two hundred casualties, most of them open wounds, none of them trivial. The staff of St Martin's stood up to this ordeal magnificently and no word of praise is high enough for them. There was no panic, no fear, no haste. Everything went on smoothly and the injured people, many of them in great pain, were handled delicately and quietly. As far as I know a similar number of casualties to those with which we dealt were also admitted and treated at the RUH.

Anyone who has endured an air raid knows what a traumatic experience it is, and one that will never be forgotten. To be huddled helplessly in the pitch-darkness of a damp shelter or under a staircase with family and friends, listening to the incessant roar of aircraft overhead, the whistle of falling bombs, the rattle of machine-gun and 'cough' of cannon fire, and the shouts and screams of those outside in the thick of it is a terrifying experience. In a sad reflection on human nature, one of the present authors, whose home was near Julian Road during the blitz, recalls that even in such tragic circumstances looting took place. A warden

This house adjacent to St Mary's Roman Catholic Church at the bottom of Burlington Street received a direct hit. Air Raid Warden Alexander MacDougall (seventy-eight) of 13 Rivers Street was killed while sheltering in the doorway of the house. All of his personal possessions were stolen.

who was killed while sheltering in the doorway of a house that suffered a direct hit at the bottom of Burlington Street had all his personal possessions stolen.

'Would they come again?' was the question on everyone's lips that Sunday. Many decided that they would not wait to find out. That day an estimated 10,000 inhabitants locked up their homes and with some provisions and a few belongings left the city for the relative safety of Hampton Rocks and Sally-in-the-Woods, or to stay with friends or relatives in neighbouring towns and villages.

The raiders did come again. In the early hours of Monday 27 April the sirens wailed and at 1.25 a.m. eighty-three German bombers rained their destruction of 107 tonnes of high explosive and nearly 8,000 incendiary bombs onto the city for the third time in two days. Many of the bombers dived low over the city to deliver their bomb loads and then machine-gunned the streets as they withdrew. Much of the area bounded by the Assembly Rooms, Lansdown Road and Julian Road bore the brunt of this night's attack. Four city churches – St John's, St James's, St Andrew's and Holy Trinity – were either completely destroyed or seriously damaged that night, and at the Regina Hotel in Bennett Street twenty-seven people died when the establishment received a direct hit.

RAF nightfighter Beaufighters, Defiants and Hurricanes from Middle Wallop, Exeter, Colerne and Charmy Down had better luck that night, engaging several German bombers over the city. Nine combats ensued but only one enemy aircraft was destroyed: a Dornier Do 17 was damaged by an 87 Squadron Hurricane from Charmy Down over Lansdown and crashed into the sea on its return flight. The *Chronicle* of 27 April told Bathonians what most of them already knew:

St Andrew's Church ablaze at the height of the blitz, as seen from Rivers Street.

St Andrew's Church, Julian Road, was totally gutted by incendiary bombs. The iron scrollwork is all that remains of the great west door. (Bath Reference Library)

Heavy Death Roll in Second Big Bath Raid

For the second night in succession Bath took the brunt of the Nazi vengeance for RAF raids last night. For two hours bombers rained their loads of destruction on the city and swept the streets with machine-gun fire after first lighting the city up with a shower of flares.

It is feared the death roll will be heavy. A large number of casualties were caused by a direct hit on a shelter. Incendiary bombs started serious fires.

Though the raid was on a considerably smaller scale than on the previous night – it lasted only two hours – it is thought that bigger bombs were used, and damage is said to be extensive. British night fighters were in action, and it is known that three raiders which crossed were destroyed. A number of others were so severely damaged that they are unlikely to have reached their bases. Over Nazi aerodromes in France, British fighters patrolled the skies and harassed the raiders as they returned.

Many of the battles in the sky were fought over and around Bath, and streams of incendiary bullets were seen as our fighters came into contact with the raiders. The Air Ministry states that elsewhere in the West and South-West damage done by the raiders was slight, and no casualties have so far been reported.

Historic buildings, churches, a hospital and business premises suffered severely. At one hospital Bristol surgeons worked throughout the night dealing with casualties. Ambulances were augmented by private cars. Outside one

Abbey Church House in Westgate Buildings was badly damaged in the Saturday raid.
The portrait of an Abbey rector still hangs on a wall (centre).

historic building was a pathetic relic of Beau Nash days – a sedan chair, covered with dust, but intact. The façade of one famous crescent, a Georgian gem, was badly damaged. In many streets were pathetic bundles of belongings, sometimes piled on perambulators or carts. Three children made their way through the city, bravely carrying their all in a tin bath! In one badly hit area two Union Jacks fluttered defiance from the wreckage of a bed which lay in the street.

This front-page report seems to make light of what had been the most devastating event in the history of the City of Bath. However, newspaper editors were under great pressure from the Government not to give away too many details of the results of enemy action, for fear of handing the Germans raid intelligence on a plate and undermining public morale.

Material damage was enormous and loss of life was great. Whole families had been wiped out, complete neighbourhoods devastated. In the days that followed, Weymouth House School was used for a temporary mortuary as bodies continued to be pulled from the rubble of bomb damaged buildings. Stunned Bathonians read the names of the dead from lists that were posted at regular intervals on a notice-board outside the school and at the ARP headquarters in Broad Street. Identification of the dead was a heart-breaking experience for relatives and friends alike. In two sobering public ceremonies one week after the raids, hundreds of blitz victims were buried in two mass graves on the windswept slopes of Haycombe Cemetery over-looking the Englishcombe valley.

An Army field kitchen is used by Bath policemen to prepare meals for bombed-out families in the aftermath of the blitz.

Devastation at Lansdown Place East. The chequered flag denoted the presence of a possible unexploded bomb. (Bath Reference Library)

One week later the King and Queen toured the devastated city and talked to its inhabitants. One of the present authors remembers the Royal party standing near the gutted shell of the Assembly Rooms. After the Queen had remarked 'I think you're all wonderful!' a woman in the crowd called out, 'We can take it your Majesty, we can take it!' Whereupon a man shouted 'We've bloody well got to!'

The full story of the carnage that took place within the City of Bath on those two fateful nights in April 1942 was not revealed to its citizens until 1944, when details of the 400 blitz dead and the 19,000 buildings destroyed or damaged were published in the *Chronicle*. By then more than two years had passed since the raids and the authorities considered that Bath was now 'a safe area from the point of view of aerial attack'.

A rare view of the bomb damaged city taken by an RAF reconnaissance aircraft on the morning of 27 April 1942. (RAF photo/Bath Reference Library)

BATH BLITZ CASUALTIES, APRIL 1942

Killed and injured – 1,272
Deaths (inc. died in hospital and missing) – 400
  151 men, 188 women, 61 children under 16
Seriously wounded and admitted to hospital – 357
  177 men, 156 women, 24 children
Slightly wounded – 515
  308 men, 174 women, 33 children
Bombed-out but uninjured – more than 2,600

A more permanent record of Bath's victims is contained in a beautifully inscribed *Book of Remembrance* kept in the Abbey. It lists the names of over 400 civilians and men and women of the Armed Forces who were killed in the Bath raids.

Men of the city's two Home Guard battalions, aided by soldiers from the Welsh Guards and the Royal Engineers, joined forces with Civil Defence workers in dozens of rescue operations across the city. There were many acts of great bravery in Bath both during and in the immediate aftermath of the raids, and for two of these deeds the George Medal was later awarded (the George Medal was the 'junior' award to the George Cross, the 'civilian VC'); other awards were presented for outstanding devotion to duty.

Reginald Willey, a member of the Keynsham Civil Defence Rescue Service, received his George Medal for 'great courage and endurance' after the Circus Tavern was demolished by bombs and people were trapped under the debris. Tunnelling into the wreckage Willey worked in cramped conditions for three hours, in great danger of explosions from nearby bombs and falling debris, to free those who were trapped. 'It is due to his efforts that the lives of two people were saved', concluded the official citation.

Opposite the Assembly Rooms, at the scene of devastation that was once the Regina Hotel, partly demolished in the Sunday raid by a direct hit from a single high explosive bomb, more than twenty guests were killed and many more wounded. 'For conspicuous gallantry in carrying out work in a very brave manner' Company Sergeant Major James Leslie of 6th Somerset (Bath Admiralty) Battalion, Home Guard, was also awarded the George Medal.

Some months later the *Chronicle* related the bravery of Sergeant Bert Brown of the 5th Somerset (Bath City) Battalion, Home Guard, who was awarded the British Empire Medal (BEM) for heroism at Bear Flat during the blitz. Brown, who had served in the First World War, had won the Military Medal at Ypres:

The pitiful remains of the Regina Hotel, Bennett Street, in which twenty-seven people were killed. Note the white band painted on the lamp-post and the bin containing sand for use in fighting fires. (Bath Reference Library)

Mr V. Sellar, whose drapery establishment and home – the same building – on the Bear Flat received a direct hit, told a 'Chronicle and Herald' reporter: 'My wife, two daughters, girl billetee and myself were sheltering under the dining room table when the upper part of the building fell. The three girls managed to get out and tried unsuccessfully to move a piece of masonry which was pinning me down. Hearing footsteps outside we all shouted, but the steps faded away. Presently, however, the man came back. He was Sergt. B. Brown, of Odd Down. He apologised for not having come at once but explained that he had been carrying a wounded comrade to

Spectators at Bear Flat survey the bomb damage. (Bath Reference Library)

AWARDS AND DECORATIONS FOR BRAVERY IN THE BLITZ, APRIL 1942

George Medal (GM) – R.N. Willey, Civil Defence (CD); Warrant Officer J.A. Leslie, 6th Bn Home Guard.
Order of the British Empire (OBE) – H.P. Hind, Chief Constable and ARP Controller.
Member of the British Empire (MBE) – Mrs M.J. Whimster, WVS; Major G.D. Lock, Chief Warden, CD.
British Empire Medal (BEM) – Private T. Cheeseborough, Pioneer Corps; Sergeant B. Brown, 5th Bn Home Guard; Mrs J.M. Woolmer, Ambulance Driver; Privates N.W.S. Baker, J.M. Martell and H.D. Rees, 6th Bn Home Guard.
Commendations from HM the King for Brave Conduct in Civil Defence – W. Derrick, Member, CD Rescue Service; A.J. Moody, Senior Warden, CD Warden's Service; S.E. Van den Broek, Despatch Rider, CD Rescue Service; Corporal E.E. Webb, Home Guard; S.L. Bailey, Special Constable; G.H. Lynham and W. Rawlings, Wardens, CD Warden's Service; Mrs M.J. Whimster, WVS; P.H. Bray, Supervisor, 2/6 Rescue Party, CD Rescue Service, Keynsham.

Demolition of bomb damaged buildings in Newark Street, now the site of the bus station. In the background the flag of St George flutters defiantly from the tower of the Abbey.

safety. Bombs were bursting all around and machine gun bullets flying, but he remained cool as a cucumber. He lifted the masonry off my chest and I was then able to help him to release my wife. He escorted us to the shelter, left his coat for one of my daughters who was wearing only night clothing, then he disappeared. I had to make numerous enquiries before I could find out who he was and write to thank him.' Sergt. Brown's only comment was a modest 'I simply did my duty'.

Josephine Woolmer, an ambulance driver, was the only woman to receive an award for gallant conduct during the Bath raids:

An Ambulance Depot received a direct hit from a bomb and the telephone operator was injured. The telephone room was almost in ruins but it was found that communications could be maintained. An unexploded time-bomb was lying in a corner near the telephone but, despite this, Mrs Woolmer volunteered to attend to the switchboard as telephone operator, which she did for a period of half an hour. During this time messages were received and ambulances and First Aid Parties despatched to incidents. When the telephone finally became useless, Mrs Woolmer left the Depot intending to re-establish telephonic communication with Control. When this failed she continued to act throughout the raid as an ambulance driver.

The work of rebuilding Bath was a protracted one and bombed sites were still to be seen many years after the war. In 1944 the cost of making good the material damage to the city was expected to exceed £1.3 million. The memory of those terrible events lingers on . . .

CHAPTER 6

'Your Chance to Beat the Enemy'

WAR SAVINGS

Fighting a world war was an expensive business, not just in terms of human lives and property, but also financially. With the cost of the war running into millions of pounds each day, the British Government set up the War Savings Campaign in February 1940 to raise money from the public to feed the war machine. Spurred on by an advertising budget greater even than that available to the Ministry of Food, the ethic of saving for the national good was promoted to the British public with promises of victory tomorrow in return for a little hardship today. In a fit of patriotic fervour, the nation set forth in a flurry of savings activities. At their height in 1943, 300,000 savings groups – street groups, works groups, school groups, etc. – were active up and down the country and had raised a staggering £2,777 million by the end of the war.

In March 1940 it was proudly announced that the citizens of Bath had invested £21,637 in Defence Bonds and in May the *Chronicle* carried a photograph showing children at Widcombe Junior School handing over their pennies 'which before the war they used to expend in the purchase of sweets'.

On sale in some Bath shops were 'Save for Victory' scarves, one of which was purchased from Walker & Ling, the drapers and milliners in Milsom Street, by the famous popular singer Gracie Fields. She was snapped by the *Chronicle* photographer as she made her purchase: '"By gum its gradely", our Gracie seems to be saying', ran the caption. By the late summer of 1940 Bath led the way in National Savings and the authorities wanted to know 'how the city does it'. In September 1942 the *Chronicle* was able to report that Bath had saved over £3.5 million in twenty months – a huge sum of money from a city with a population of just 70,000.

Savings were just one way in which capital was raised for the war effort. To the man and woman in the street the War Savings Scheme – an extension of the prewar National Savings Movement – made good common sense and appealed to their sense of patriotism. In any case, as the war progressed the shortage of everything from luxury goods to petrol

Our fighting men are ready — at sea, on land, and in the air. The men and women in our munition plants are working day and night.

Now comes the full opportunity for you to help with all the means in your power.

This issue of National War Bonds provides a great channel through which the full financial power of the Nation can be poured continuously — at full pressure.

Buy Bonds now and keep on buying them month by month.

2½% National War Bonds
1945-47
Unlimited Issue – Continuously "on tap"

A full Trustee Security — Price of issue £100 per cent — Subscriptions of £100 or multiples of £100 will be received until further notice — Interest accrues from date of purchase — Prospectus and application forms obtainable from Banks or Stockbrokers.

Investment in War Bonds was seen as an ideal way to help the war effort. This advertisement from 1940 is typical of those that appeared at regular intervals in the newspapers.

START A SAVINGS GROUP IN YOUR STREET

Help in the fight by forming a Savings Group in your street, factory or office. Get in touch with the Hon. Secretary of your local Savings Committee, he will give you full particulars. The Post Office has his name and address

National Savings groups were soon set up all over the country with enthusiastic collectors in offices, factories and residential areas.

meant that it was hard for people to spend money. But to the Government, war savings also acted as an effective brake on inflation.

In the 1940 Budget, increased taxes 'which will pay for Victory' were announced on a range of goods and services, and were seen by the people as a less palatable way in which to help the war effort. Beer went up by 1*d* a pint; there was an extra 1*s* 9½*d* on a bottle of Scotch and 3*d* on an ounce of tobacco. Letter postage was raised to 2½*d* and telephone charges by 15 per cent. Not content with these increases, the Government went further and imposed a new purchase tax 'to limit expenditure'.

As the threat of invasion began to build in the summer of 1940, the Mayoress of Bath's 'Shilling Fund for a Spitfire' was launched in July. With the Battle of Britain beginning to gather momentum, a target sum of £5,000 was set and on the first day more than 1,700 subscribers gave 'thousands of shillings', spurred on by the slogan 'to keep your name off the bomb, put it on the Spitfire'. The spirit of patriotism was running high and the target was easily exceeded. A cheque for £5,443 18*s* 6*d* was handed over to the Ministry of Aircraft Production in September, when the Battle of Britain was in full flight and raging in the skies over southern England. Money was also raised by exhibiting a few of the hundreds of German aircraft that had been shot down during the Battle. In October a Messerschmitt Bf 109 single-seat fighter that had been brought down near Canterbury was displayed on the Recreation Ground.

In November 1941, in recognition of the sum of money raised in the previous year by the city's Spitfire appeal fund, the Mayor of Bath received a plaque with the inscription:

In the hour of peril, citizens of Bath earned the gratitude of the British nations sustaining the valour of the Royal Air Force and fortifying the cause of Freedom by the gift of a Spitfire aircraft. They shall mount up with wings as eagles. Issued by the Ministry of Aircraft Production, 1941.

The year 1941 also marked the beginning of a succession of appeal campaigns in Bath that continued until the end of the war. Mirroring campaigns across the nation, each had a different theme and the first was 'War Weapons Week', which ran from 15 to 22 February. It was opened officially by the First Sea Lord and had a target of £500,000, representing 'one destroyer, two tanks and one bomber'. Encouraged by the slogan 'Lend to Win', people donated £200,000 on the first

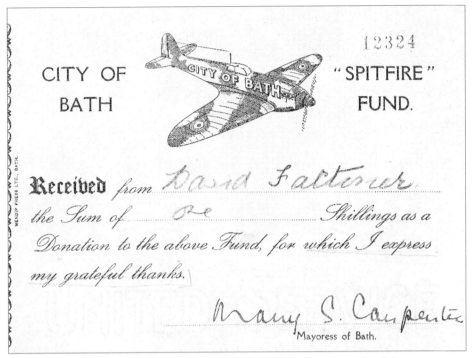

Every Little Counts: this receipt records the donation of 1s to the Spitfire Fund from six-year-old David Falconer, one of the authors. (Authors)

day alone and, to maintain the momentum, a Hurricane fighter gave a spirited display to members of Bath Home Guard on Lansdown, a real boost to the week.

Bath's next major fundraising campaign was 'Bath Warship Week' in 1942 with a target of £750,000 'necessary for the provision of three equipped destroyers'. 'Warship Week' was launched on 21 November and three days later the amount raised stood at nearly £300,000. By 1 December the target had been exceeded by more than £40,000, with the *Chronicle* reporting that 'a final spurt did it!'. As a result of 'Warship Week', the City of Bath and the Rural District of Bathavon each officially adopted a Royal Navy warship: HMS *Jervis* – a 'J' Class fleet destroyer; and HMS *Beaufort* – a 'Hunt' Class escort destroyer. Both ships survived the war.

In December 1942 plans were announced to buy aeroplanes in another huge nationwide campaign. As part of a national savings drive held between March and July 1943, cities, towns and villages across the nation staged 'Wings for Victory' appeals in bids to raise money to buy aircraft for the RAF. Bath's 'Wings for Victory Week' ran from 3 to 10 April, and to help the fundraising along a Spitfire fighter was installed in the Sawclose where it was on view to the public throughout the week. The *Chronicle* of 2 April 1943 carried an advertisement that read: 'Spitfire on your target Bath, tomorrow's our great day. Bath must save £800,000 to win its victory wings.' Three days later the paper reminded readers that: 'Your stamps will speed 500lb bomb which will be loaded and dropped on Germany. It [the unarmed bomb] is standing in the vestibule of the Beau Nash cinema waiting for you to stick on as many savings stamps as space permits.'

Nearly on Target! A model Spitfire trailing a streamer over the roof of the Guildhall near the end of the campaign recording 'Towards £5,000'.

Four days later the 'Wings' total stood at £676,704 and by the end of the week Bath had won its wings with a tremendous total of £911,061 raised – 'and more to come!'. One Bath lady alone gave £1,000 to the Spitfire fund. The Spitfire in the Sawclose had done its bit for 'Wings Week', and was dismantled and taken away by an RAF maintenance unit team 'with the help of a mobile petrol-driven crane and an assumingly outsize lorry'. When the final figure was announced on 16 April, it was revealed that Bath had raised a magnificent £920,453 and a plaque in recognition of this great feat was presented to the city fathers by a grateful Air Ministry. By the end of the four-month campaign on 3 July, a grand total of £615,945,000 had been raised in Great Britain, representing a £70.3 million increase on the similar 'Warships Week' campaign of 1942.

On 1 June 1944 Bath's next campaign was announced. It was to be called 'Salute the Soldier Week' and would run from 3 to 10 June. 'Our target three squadrons of Churchill tanks costing £900,000, but make it a million and beat all records' challenged the official programme to the week's events. At the end of the first day of fundraising, the total- to-date indicator in the Abbey Churchyard registered the amazing sum of £141,064 but 'we must not relax' the War Minister told the Mayor, Councillor Joseph Plowman.

As Bathonians settled down to another day's work in offices, shops, factories and homes across the city on the morning of Tuesday 6 June, the startling news bulletin issued from Supreme Headquarters Allied Expeditionary Force at 9.33 a.m. turned the day into a date with destiny:

Left: '*Bath Warship Week*' *ran from 22 to 29 November 1941 with a target figure of £750,000 'to purchase a fully-equipped destroyer*'. Right, top: *Capt H.F. Farr RN gave his contribution to Rodney's collecting basket on the steps of the Guildhall. Rodney was owned by Miss Mabel Eastham.* Right, bottom: *The 'Wings for Victory' campaign in 1943 aimed to raise the sum of £800,000.*

Under the command of General Eisenhower, Allied Naval Forces, supported by strong Air Forces, began landing Allied armies on the north coast of France.

The Second Front had opened at last and on that same day, Bath's 'Salute the Soldier' total stood at nearly half a million pounds. With the reassuring report on 10 June that the British front in Normandy was solid from Bayeux to Isigny, came the equally good news that Bath had smashed its 'Salute' target. That evening revellers danced the night away to Reg Ball and his Band at the Pavilion and Arthur Clark and his Band at the Pump Room, safe in the knowledge that enough money had been raised to equip three squadrons of Churchill tanks for the British Army. With the tough battles of the Normandy beachhead still to come, those tanks were going to come in very useful.

Programme BATH *Price 3d.*
SALUTES THE SOLDIER
June   3-10

Bath's 'Salute the Soldier Week' ran from 3 to 10 June 1944 with a target figure of £900,000, but citizens were urged to 'make it a million' – which they did. (Authors)

This was the final fund raising campaign for the war effort in Bath. By early in 1945, an Allied victory was virtually assured and people were turning their attention to 'peace-day' celebrations and postwar plans for the city.

BATH'S SALVAGE SCHEME

National salvage drives were an important feature of the war years and went hand in hand with the theme of thrift extolled in the War Savings Campaign. With the Battle of the Atlantic being fought against Hitler's U-boats, which were taking a heavy toll on Allied merchant shipping convoys, the more self-sufficient Britain could become, the less foodstuffs and raw materials would need to be shipped in from overseas.

Answering the call for salvage, local salvage shops and street depots were set up for the collection of scrap iron, bones, waste paper, aluminium pots and pans and countless other items that could be recycled for the war effort. Even kitchen waste was processed and fed to pigs.

By the spring of 1941 some 12,000 Bath householders were aiding the Salvage Scheme and the city took top place among county boroughs for general salvage collection. The City Engineer's Department that managed the scheme told householders:

Bath is selling 16 tons of cooked food waste weekly (enough to feed 250 pigs) but we could dispose of 70 tons! Will you please help us to reach this total?

Remember, every scrap of foodstuff saved is a blow to Hitler's U-boats which are out to starve us. Here is your chance to beat the enemy in your kitchen. Put your reply to Hitler's threat in the waste food bin.

Bath has placed in the streets bins for the reception of waste food. You are earnestly requested to save all suitable kitchen waste and place it in the nearest street bin to your house. Put your wrapping or other container in the sack which will be found near the bin. Make a practice of doing this frequently. Do not leave all your waste for the week-end. This will ensure that it will be collected at least twice a week, and will reach the Central Depot in a fresh condition.

Save your waste and help Britain to make sure of bacon, eggs and Victory!

In the drive for scrap metal, the city's Salvage Scheme operators asked Bathonians to have a good look round for old razor blades, scrap iron, disused grates and garden railings – the latter 'merely make the garden look smaller and cost money for painting', they reassured householders, adding generously that 'the Council will remove them free of cost'.

TWELVE MONTHS' WORK

WASTE PAPER

SCRAP IRON

1,045 TONS This is returned to the paper mills to be pulped and re-used for munitions and industrial purposes. Light your fires with dirty, greasy or grease-proof paper which is not wanted for pulping. If you are not already a contributor ask your dustman for a sack and prepaid postcard

442 TONS Iron enough to make 177 guns

RAGS

BONES

34 TONS Returned to Textile industry through the mills for the Army, R.A.F. Blue, khaki and export trade; some is used for munitions

28 TONS Makes explosives, glues, fertilizers, etc. Bath school-children have responded well in their school bone collections

BOTTLES & JARS

TINS

150,385 Returned to Industry and Commerce

252 TONS Flattened and returned to steel works

ALUMINIUM POTS & PANS

MISCELLANEOUS
Rubber, curled hair, old batteries, gramophone records, old string, rabbit skins, etc.

18 CWT For war-planes. A gift to the Ministry of Aircraft Production

20 TONS Each plays a varied and important part in the War and Industrial effort of the Country

YOU CAN DO MORE THAN YOU IMAGINE TO SPEED THE VICTORY!

★ The best thanks of this Department are due to all who have helped to make the scheme a success, with a special tribute to Mrs. Whimster and all members of the Women's Voluntary Services who have so ably worked for us since its inception. We are indebted to Mr. W. Heath Robinson for his interest in our Bath Scheme. His method, however, is a bit too ambitious for Bath, but we hope you will show the same enthusiasm for saving waste foodstuff as the householders in his drawing, and bring it regularly to your nearest street bin.

Designed and Printed by Dawson & Goodall Ltd, Grove Street, Bath

CITY OF BATH SALVAGE SCHEME FOR
WASTE FOOD AND WASTE MATERIALS

This Salvage Scheme leaflet was issued to all Bath households in April 1941 by the City Engineer. It was backed up by regular newspaper advertisements. (Authors)

A salvage collection point in the Circus.

In retrospect, one of the most disturbing aspects of the scheme was the removal of antique iron railings from Bath's squares and crescents of historic buildings. The suburban areas of Bath suffered equally from the drive for scrap metal, with dozens of iron garden railings being removed from homes across the city, from Larkhall to Bear Flat. Overall, the city suffered particularly badly in this respect and it is only in recent years that some of these railings have been replaced. Compensation was offered by the Ministry of Supply, but no appeal was allowed.

Among other serious losses to the city's heritage were two historic Russian cannon standing east and west of the obelisk in Victoria Park, captured by the British Army at Sebastapol in 1855 during the Crimean War. They were removed in 1942 to make munitions for use in 'the fight against the Huns' and the gun carriages were broken up for the same purpose. In 1943, when Bath was ordered to pull up the tram rails for scrap, the Chairman of the Surveying Committee said he was 'out to create a rumpus if the government did not agree to treat the city equitably in the matter of finance'.

In the same year manuscripts of music specially composed for the Bath Pageant in 1909 were put out for salvage. Fortunately, a vigilant member of the city library staff rescued them for the Reference Library collection. One cannot help but wonder how many other items of historic interest disappeared in the frantic wartime drive for salvage.

The caption to this photograph in the Chronicle *reads: 'IT'S POTS AND PANS – that will go a long way towards winning this war. Any quantity of aluminium articles will be welcomed at the depot of the Women's Voluntary Service, No. 8 Quiet St., Bath, where this picture was taken.'*

CHAPTER 7
Food and Rationing

FOOD RATIONING

Before the war as much as 60 per cent of Britain's food had come from abroad, as well as raw materials for industry. As early as July 1939, in anticipation of the outbreak of war, the Government had issued a public information leaflet entitled 'Your Food in Wartime' in which it explained what had been done so far to safeguard food supplies, how traders and householders could help, what to do about emergency supplies in case of evacuation, local distribution and a proposed rationing scheme. On New Year's Day 1940 the Ministry of Food placed advertisements in newspapers telling people to register immediately for meat that would shortly be rationed, and later that month food rationing was introduced throughout the country.

Rationing brought some degree of fairness to the way people obtained food and ensured that everyone could be certain of getting their share of basic necessities. Coupons as well as money were now required to buy essential goods that were then in short supply. According to availability and at different times of the war, some foodstuffs came on and off ration.

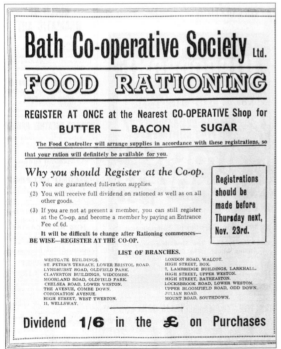

Bath Co-operative Society advertisement in the Chronicle *encouraging residents to register with one of their branches for butter, bacon and sugar.*

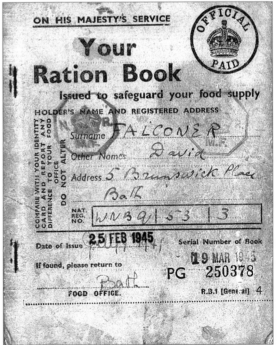

The ration book issued to David Falconer, one of the authors, in February 1945. (Authors)

Goods that came to Britain from Asia, Australia, Africa and America had to be brought across the oceans in merchant convoys escorted by the British and Commonwealth Navies. German U-boats, surface raiders and aircraft did their best to attack and sink these vital convoys and it became increasingly difficult to maintain supplies of raw materials like timber and iron, and foods like meat, cheese, butter and oranges. As the Germans tightened the noose on Britain's Atlantic supply lines, the pressure grew ever greater on her civilian population to tighten their belts and become as self-sufficient as possible. Germany came close to winning the so-called Battle of the Atlantic and starving Britain into submission; but thanks to Allied sea and air power, assisted by scientific developments that helped in the detection of U-boats, the Germans lost their grip on the noose – but only just.

Far away from this desperate battle being fought on and beneath the waves of the unforgiving Atlantic Ocean, the war to ensure everyone had enough to eat was also being fought on the home front. The nerve-centre of food rationing in Bath was at the Food Office situated in the fine Octagon building in Milsom Street. Here officials seated at trestle tables controlled Bath's food supply with one third of a million ration sheets. Citizens were urged to register with shops as soon as they received their new ration books.

Rationing regulations were strictly enforced and the *Chronicle* carried regular reports of the many attempts by people in Bath to 'buck' the system. In a rare case brought before Bath Police Court in April 1941 a woman resident in Weston Road, who was doing war work in the city, was fined £2 for obtaining meat unlawfully from her sister in Ireland. The discovery was made by the censor's office, which intercepted a letter to the woman. In August a Bath grocer found himself in court for overcharging on butter and jam, and then there were the 'artful dodgers' as the *Chronicle* reported:

Three clerks at the Food Control Office in the Octagon make a final check of ration books. 'Everything is now in readiness for rationing if, and when the Government orders it.'

Some housewives are using simple disguises to deceive shopkeepers into supplying them twice or three times with unrationed foodstuffs. After the first purchase they don dark glasses, or remove hats and coats to rejoin the queue. The authorities are considering the possibility of false pretences charges.

It was believed, though, that the 'queue habit', largely confined to the weekend, was on the wane. A reporter noted:

Queues were usually associated with the desire for such comestibles as cakes, biscuits, sausages and sweets. There is certainly no need whatever to queue for essential foods like meat, fish and vegetables, which are plentiful. Yet I have seen women lining up at a butcher's shop, also at a fish shop, when there was no need for it in either case. This occurred in the early morning, and in the evening there were still good supplies of meat and fish in both establishments.

Milk, a staple of a wholesome diet, was rationed because production had fallen due to the 'plough-up' policy for agriculture. In 'Today's Food News' in the *Chronicle* of 25 August 1942, people were told that 'from next week until the end of October the allowance for all non-priority consumers will average 3 pints a week'. The following summer there was a review of milk distribution in Bath and people were warned that transport difficulties could mean milkless days. A new distribution scheme designed to save petrol, tyres and labour came into operation on 25 July 1943. Seventy-five dairymen were involved, and 35,361 registrations were 'parcelled out' among them. However, the new scheme did not find favour with some people and there was at least one disgruntled customer. Mr Charles Kettley of Albany Road, Twerton, when told that he would be placed on the list of a new retailer, retorted that he had been dealing with the same milkman since 3 October 1880 and he did not care to change at his time of life!

Eggs were brought under a scheme of controlled distribution ensuring adequate supplies for 'priority' consumers in June 1941. In August 1943 it was reported that new suppliers of eggs were wanted and there had been a rush to change traders. Long queues of serious looking people, mainly women, had been observed at the Food Office 'doggedly determined to change their retailers, although not too pleased at the prospect of a long wait'.

Oranges, brought in at great cost by our merchant seamen, were usually in short supply. A traditional fruit at Christmastide, oranges were sorely missed, but the *Chronicle* reported during the run-up to the festive season in 1943 that there was a possibility of a supply being available shortly:

Cookery demonstrations at the Gas Showrooms in Old Bond Street, and 'Food Facts' published at regular intervals in the Chronicle, *suggested ways of ekeing out meagre wartime rations and helped people prepare interesting and appetising dishes.*

Enjoying a wartime lunch in 1942 on the terrace above the Roman Baths. The man wearing the wing-collar and facing the camera at the first table is Mr John Hatton, Spa Director.

These, if not specially for children, are available for sale on production of ration books. Many suppliers find that people come in from the surrounding country, even from Bristol, and as retailers cannot refuse to sell so long as ration books are shown, it sometimes happens that they have no supplies left when their regular customers arrive later.

Bath people were nothing if not ingenious in their efforts to minimise the hardships caused by food shortages and rationing. In June 1941 voluntary women workers set up a new initiative known as the Bath Homegrown Fruit Canvas, which planned seven jam 'factories' for the city. The women went from door to door collecting surplus fruit for making into jam, which was then sold to the public through retailers.

Even in those austere war years, humour was seldom absent from the pages of the local newspaper. At strategic points in the city, large iron static water tanks were installed as an aid to firefighting. In September 1942 the *Chronicle* carried a cartoon entitled 'Brighter Bath 3' depicting a static water tank in which a duck is swimming. The caption reads: 'Keep duck on static water and increase food supplies.'

Food rationing did not cease with the end of the war. In fact it became worse with the introduction of bread rationing (not rationed during the war) and did much to add to the misery of the postwar austerity years. Not until the mid-1950s was food rationing in Britain finally abolished.

One of Bath's two Ford emergency food vans pictured on Cleveland Bridge in September 1943. (Kingsmead Motor Co.)

FOOD CATERING

From early in the war a number of schemes were established for supplying food and providing meals in the city, some of them to be activated only in time of emergency such as air raids, invasion and evacuation. Among the earliest was the lunch club for civil servants opened in April 1940 in the Assembly Rooms where, on the first two days, 250 lunches were served at 1s 3d per head. On offer was a varied menu from which patrons could choose:

In July 1940 the Mayor of Bath made appeals for donations to establish mobile canteens in the city and a little over a year later, in September 1941, two food vans were delivered to the Kingsmead Motor Company. These were part of a fleet of 350 vehicles presented to Britain by Henry Ford to help with emergency feeding following air raids. In November the two Ford vans, manned by WVS drivers and attendants, served 4d dinners in Bath schools.

By the autumn of 1940 temporary feeding stations for use following an air raid had been established at locations all over the city: the Salvation Army Hall, Abbey Church House, St Luke's Parish Hall, old St Bartholomew's Church, St Mary's Church Hall in Grove Street, Walcot Methodist School Room, St Stephen's Church House, Weston Adult School and Twerton Baptist Room – the latter for temporary use only. To cover the influx of evacuees to the city, a reception centre providing food and shelter was set up at St Paul's Mission in Corn Street. In Northgate Street, members of the armed forces could enjoy a cup of tea at the Bath Red Shield Club Hostel. During the first year of war the YMCA in Broad Street provided a day and night canteen that served 12,000 men with breakfast, tea, supper and snacks.

THE BRITISH RESTAURANTS

In 1941 plans were afoot to open three 'British Restaurants' in Bath. Although the name of these establishments was coined by Winston Churchill, the restaurants had been first proposed by the Chamberlain Cabinet early in 1940. This was in response to complaints from the general public about the availability of luxury foods served in many up-market hotels and restaurants that snapped up supplies of good quality unrationed foodstuffs. If the better off could enjoy the privilege of eating well 'off the ration', then why couldn't the ordinary working man and woman? Churchill objected to the Ministry of Food's proposed name, 'Communal Feeding Centres', which he regarded 'as an odious expression suggestive of Communism and the workhouse'.

In July 1941 the *Chronicle* announced that the Ministry of Food would take any profits from the restaurants but would also make good any losses. It would appear that initially the Pavilion was considered for use as the central restaurant, while two others would be located at Oldfield Park and Walcot. It was envisaged that 'a good square meal' would be available for the modest sum of 7*d* or 8*d*. A meat and two veg course would cost 5*d* or 6*d*, soup with bread 2*d*, and for a similar sum the meal could be rounded off with a pudding.

In the following February a scheme to build the three restaurants was approved and work begun at Charlotte Street car park, at Kensington on tennis courts formerly used by the Post Office Sports Club, and at Cotswold Road, just off Monksdale Road in Oldfield Park adjoining the Council playing fields. The total cost of constructing and equipping the three restaurants was estimated at £16,421 and until work was completed the Pavilion was used as a temporary restaurant. In July 1942 the *Chronicle* was gratified to note that since the Pavilion had opened as a British Restaurant, not one piece of cutlery had been lost or stolen.

The citizens of Bath were invited to submit their ideas for suitable names for the three new restaurants and those submitting the winning entries would be awarded prizes. In August the following names were chosen: Parkside for Charlotte Street, Riverside for Kensington, and Hillside for Oldfield Park. By the beginning of 1943 Parkside was paying well and there was growing use of the other two restaurants. Parkside, the first of the three to open, claimed to serve twelve meals every minute. 'Smooth service, cleanliness and good value sums up briefly our aim at Parkside British Restaurant' reported the *Chronicle*.

In the autumn of 1943 plans were discussed to open Parkside BR every evening during the winter, including Sundays, as a meeting place for young people. The aim was to provide an alternative to the attractions of street corners and public houses, where many Bath youth were perceived to be idling their time away at night. Sadly, however, as is too often the case, good intentions that would have benefited many were ruined by the selfish actions of a few. The *Chronicle* of 17 February 1944 noted:

Tough guys and gang conflicts

The question of whether or not the 'open house' experiment is to continue either at the present premises – the Parkside BR – or elsewhere, caused a long discussion at the meeting on Wednesday of the Bath Education Committee. Apparently there was a lot of rowdyism at the BR every night. The evening visitors include about 12 tough specimens from certain gangs, and other gangs get into conflict with one another.

Nationally, 2,160 British Restaurants had opened by September 1943, but this figure fell far short of the 10,000 envisaged by the Government.

DIGGING FOR VICTORY

'Dig for Victory' was one of the great wartime slogans and was launched in a radio broadcast by the Minister of Agriculture in October 1939. The campaign emphasised the important part private gardens could play in food production and the public were also asked to save edible waste for pigs – 'but don't waste food'. The message was simple: the more self-sufficient Britain could become, the less space would need to be taken up in merchant shipping convoys with foodstuffs at the expense of vital war goods. As an exhortation to grow more food the public were also alerted to the 'Gardens versus U-boats' campaign. At this point of the war Britain was coming close to losing the Battle of the Atlantic, her supply convoys being decimated by marauding German U-boat 'Wolfpacks'. By late 1943, however, the tide had been turned against the Germans but it was a close-run thing and the threat never fully receded.

'Dig for Victory' was one of the most famous slogans of the war. This poster, designed to encourage people to grow their own fruit and vegetables, would have been a familiar sight on hoardings in streets up and down the country.

In an attempt to encourage people to grow their own vegetables, 26 acres of land in Bath were made available in February 1940 for allotments as part of the 'Dig for Victory' campaign. In July 1941 letters were printed in the *Chronicle* commenting on the proposed use of the Royal Crescent field for allotments rather than for grazing cattle, but it was not until 5 January 1942 that the City Council voted on this proposal:

Royal Crescent Fields for Allotments

Whether the pasture in front of Bath's famous Royal Crescent should be converted into wartime allotments was discussed by Bath City Council this morning. Eventually it was decided by 20 votes to 15 to utilise it in the way suggested. Fifty wartime allotments would be laid out there. The field, hitherto used for grazing, has provided a somewhat thorny topic for some months past. The Allotments Committee wanted it to be 'Dug for Victory' and many would-be plot holders living in the vicinity supported such a policy. But the Corporate Property Committee was not prepared to recommend utilisation for the production of food in this way, and was of the opinion that better use could be made of plots in the neighbourhood, also recommending that additional land should be taken in the Middle Common.

But the fate of the Royal Crescent lawn was still not sealed; in April 1944 the *Chronicle* reported that it was not to be used for allotments, subject to another discussion by the City Council, and the 'trim sward was saved again from the hands of despoilers'.

Returning to 1941, more allotments were made available in the city: in the field at the rear of Marlborough Buildings (they are still there), on the High Common, at Haute Combe abutting Newbridge Road, and Oolite Road estate at Odd Down. Although by mid-1941 there were signs that Bathonians were taking the allotments scheme more seriously, it seems that the pleadings for more people to grow their own vegetables had fallen largely on deaf ears for in December 1942 a request was made for one thousand more 'allotmenteers'. However, the interest in allotments at Bath remained so poor that land was eventually offered rent free.

Sadly, the good old wartime spirit was distinctly lacking in some Bathonians, and vegetables were sometimes pilfered from allotments and gardens, as the *Chronicle* of 22 July 1942 commented:

> Not only is it mean, but the penalties for offenders are severe. There is nothing more galling than for a gardener, professional or amateur, to find that a member of the 'light fingered fraternity' has stolen a march on him and taken away some of the crops he has worked hard to produce and looked forward to enjoying.

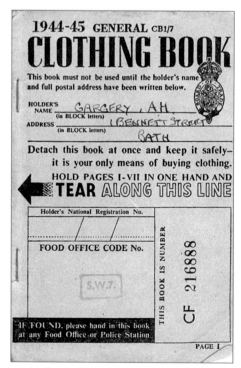

A clothing book containing Board of Trade coupons issued to A.H. Gargery, 1 Bennett Street, Bath – it was a person's only means of buying clothes during the war. (Authors)

CLOTHES RATIONING

To further stabilise the cost of living, the rationing of clothes was introduced in June 1941 along similar lines to the food rationing scheme already in place. But rather than give the customer a fixed number of coupons for one particular garment, the scheme allowed him or her to choose between a range of goods, each with a different points price. But the resources of the clothing industry under wartime conditions were insufficient to meet the original rationing levels set down by the Government.

In 1942 the clothes ration was cut further still and 'Utility clothes' were introduced. The intention behind this scheme was to standardise clothing fabrics and designs so that the hard-pressed industry could provide enough clothing at prices affordable to ordinary working-class families The design of clothes was carefully specified by the Board of Trade:

UTILITY COATS, COSTUMES & GOWNS

THIS DOES NOT MEAN A DULL & LIFELESS STANDARDISATION.

ASTUTE & CLEVER DESIGN

WITH A WIDE RANGE OF CHOICE IS THE KEYNOTE OF ALL SEASONABLE MODELS AT

Marys'

15 MILSOM STREET, BATH

To the Air Raid Shelter

SIREN SUITS
Prices from
29/11 to
59/11
In Many Colours
and Materials
(COAT DEPT.)

WILLIAM RAYNER
THE CORRIDOR :: BATH

Utility was a 'buzz' word during the war. But utility garments did 'not mean a dull & lifeless standardisation', Marys' of Milsom Street advised potential customers in this advertisement. Siren Suits were made popular by Winston Churchill, the Prime Minister. This one for ladies was offered in 'Many Colours and Materials' by William Rayner in The Corridor.

embroidery and appliqué work on women's clothing was forbidden; men's trouser turn-ups and double cuffs were prohibited; and socks were not to exceed 9½ inches in length. (Utility clothing eventually accounted for about 80 per cent of all production.)

The legacy of clothes rationing extended into the postwar years and, like food rationing, its effects continued to be felt for some time to come.

WHAT A MAN COULD BUY ON THE CLOTHES RATION INTRODUCED IN 1942

1 pair socks every 4 months
1 pair shoes every 8 months
1 shirt every 20 months
1 vest, 1 pair pants every 2 years
1 pair trousers, 1 jacket every 2 years
1 waistcoat every 5 years
1 pullover every 5 years
1 overcoat every 7 years

CHAPTER 8

Bath's War Effort

THE WHEELS OF INDUSTRY

As was the case in many other towns and cities the length and breadth of the country, Bath's factories and mills were quickly turned over to war production after war was declared in 1939. From the heavy engineering firm of Stothert & Pitt along the Lower Bristol Road at their Victoria and Newark Works, to the precision instrument makers Horstmann Gear Company at the Newbridge and Albion Works, and from Bath Cabinet Makers at Twerton to Harbutt's Plasticine in Bathampton – all became engaged in a wide variety of design and manufacturing activities to support the Army, Navy and RAF in their bid to defeat the Axis powers and thereby save the world from tyranny.

Stothert & Pitt's design and development experience was put to good use by the Ministry of Supply, mainly in connection with tank turrets and gun mountings for the Army. The firm designed and made prototypes for nearly all the gun mountings used on British tanks during the Second World War, ranging from the 2-pounder main armament on the Cruiser and Infantry tanks widely used in the French and Western Desert campaigns, to the deadly 17-pounder as

During the war Stothert & Pitt, the long-established Bath mechanical engineering firm, turned much of its production over to the design and development of tank turrets and gun mountings. Seen here are Matilda infantry tanks in the Western Desert, fitted with Stothert & Pitt gun mountings.

MULBERRY HARBOURS

Mindful of the fact that it would take some weeks to clear the port of Cherbourg of mines following the D-Day landings, Allied planners proposed to supply and strengthen the bridgehead through two artificial harbours, which would be prefabricated in England and towed across the Channel. Rumour has it that the innovative 'Mulberry' harbours were designed by the Admiralty at Bath in Kingswood School and so called after a large Mulberry tree that grew in the school grounds.

Known by their codenames as Mulberry A and Mulberry B, each harbour was roughly the size of Dover harbour and consisted of an outer floating breakwater, an inner fixed breakwater made of concrete caissons, and four floating piers running out from the beaches to 'spud pierheads'. At these pierheads small coasters and landing craft could unload direct into waiting Army lorries, while Liberty ships and other vessels could unload their cargoes into barges and ferries. On 19 June a tremendous storm in the Channel caused serious damage to both harbours, drastically reducing their capacity

fitted later in the war to the Sherman Firefly and Challenger tanks – the only Allied tanks able to compete with the firepower of the deadly German Tigers and Panthers. S&P also designed gun mountings for the Twin Oerlikon guns and the Vickers 'K' machine-gun that were fitted to Crusader tanks on escort duty for the protection of vehicle convoys against enemy air attack.

With the presence of the Admiralty in Bath during the war, it is not surprising to learn that S&P designed and manufactured a wide range of equipment for specialist naval applications. This ranged from seaplane cradles for warships to special fixed gantry cranes and landing bridges for different types of Landing Ships and Craft. These vital pieces of heavy equipment enabled troops and vehicles to be landed successfully on the Normandy beaches on D-Day in June 1944.

How best to support the Royal Navy's desperate battle to win the war at sea preoccupied the best minds at S&P and the Admiralty, who between them designed and built the two-man human torpedo or 'Chariot' at Bath. Inspired by the Italian *Maiale* (or 'swine') human torpedo – probably so called because it was difficult to manoeuvre – the Royal Navy Chariot was a 22-foot long torpedo-shaped submersible with a detachable explosive warhead attached to its nose. It was propelled by a small motor and 'driven' by a pair of frogmen who rode astride its back. Chariots were carried in pressure-tight containers welded onto the outside of large submarines. Under cover of darkness the submarine moved in close to an enemy harbour, at which point the Chariots with their crews were released into the water and made their way, submerged, towards their target vessels. Positioned beneath the ships in harbour, one crewman from each Chariot would attach the warhead to the hull of the intended enemy ship, after which they would make good their escape out to sea (on the Chariot) where they would be picked up by their waiting parent submarine. Although only a handful of these highly dangerous operations were carried out, by some ten Chariot crews, many thousands of tons of enemy shipping was sunk during

Stothert & Pitt also designed and manufactured the two-man human torpedo for the Royal Navy. (Authors)

the Second World War, including the brand-new Italian cruiser *Ulpio Traiano* in Palermo harbour in 1943. Less glamorous, but equally indispensable in the war against the German warships and U-boats, were mine sinkers, minesweeping equipment and paravane gear (a torpedo-shaped device towed from the bow of a vessel so that the cables will cut the anchors of any moored mines).

Although S&P did not manufacture weapons or components for aircraft of the RAF, it did build and supply hundreds of concrete mixers to be used in the construction of runways at the dozens of new bomber airfields that mushroomed across eastern England, enabling Bomber Command to take the war back to the German homeland. Several thousand pumps for handling bulk aviation fuel and engine coolant were also supplied to the RAF by S&P for use on airfields.

Further along the River Avon was the Horstmann Gear Company, renowned before the war for the precision instruments produced at its Newbridge and Albion Works. With the outbreak of war, the Navy and RAF found they could utilise the delicate mechanisms produced by the firm. Although the actual designs came from top secret technical sources, a high percentage of development and production was carried out in the Bath factory.

During the Battle of Britain the RAF's Spitfires and Hurricanes were equipped with a special wireless apparatus nicknamed 'Pip Squeak' by the pilots but known officially as the Horstmann Remote Contactor Type 4. By automatically transmitting a short radio signal every minute, which was received by three ground stations, the course and position of an aircraft could be plotted minute by minute during a dogfight, thus allowing the pilot to get on with the serious

business of fighting without having to fiddle with his wireless set to let base know where he was.

Another Horstmann aid to survival in the air was a wireless remote control device for single-seat fighter aircraft – a small box with four pre-set buttons. At the push of a button it enabled the pilot to speak to his base, the weather people, ask for landing facilities, or if in trouble speak on an emergency frequency. Other precision instruments manufactured by the firm for use by the RAF were astro compasses and turn and bank indicators for aircraft night flying instrument panels.

During the dark and desperate days of the Battle of the Atlantic a radio location device named Asdic, located beneath a British warship's hull, enabled it to detect enemy submarines lurking below. The wartime Royal Navy had due cause to thank the engineering skills of Horstmann Gear Company for an ingenious stabilisation device that meant no matter how much the warship changed course, the Asdic transmitter always maintained a true bearing. Another important piece of Horstmann-made equipment was the Asdic bearing plotter, which repeated to the captain on the bridge the bearing on which the transmitter was trained.

Horstmann clocks were used in sea mines to delay firing for a period after the first magnetic impulse had been received from the target and to prevent firing from false targets. Torpedo motors were started with an igniter, thousands of which came from the Newbridge factory.

The Horstmann family suffered grievously during the Bath blitz in April 1942 when Percival Horstmann (a departmental manager at the Newbridge Works), his wife Elsie, and their only child Terence were killed in the Sunday raid.

The more traditional trades such as cabinet making also had a vital part to play in the war effort alongside the more obvious engineering concerns. Along the Lower Bristol Road at the bottom of Lansdown View was the factory of Bath Cabinet Makers. Before the First World War its skilled craftsmen had made fittings for the ill-fated liner *Titanic* and later the *Queen Mary*, now pressed into service as a troop ship on fast runs across the North Atlantic. During the First World War the Flight Works (as it became known) had been involved in the construction of military aircraft and its role in the Second World War was little different. Dispersed production methods meant that Bath Cabinet Makers was involved in the manufacture of a wide range of wooden components for the aircraft industry including: laminated wooden propellers; fuselage and tailplane sections; elevators and rudders for the Airspeed Oxford trainer and Armstrong Whitworth Albemarle glider tug and paratroop transport; wings for the legendary de Havilland Mosquito fighter-bomber; and wing and fuselage sections for Airspeed Horsa gliders that were towed to Normandy on the eve of D-Day and to Arnhem later that year, carrying hundreds of airborne troops.

Plasticine is known to many as a modelling material, made until recently by Harbutt's at their Bathampton Works, but during the war it was put to a variety of widely differing uses. Army and Navy gunners moulded it into ear plugs to protect their hearing from the deafening sound of heavy gunfire, while the Special Operations Executive (SOE) used Plasticine as a safe substitute when training its secret agents in the use of plastic explosives. Air raid precautions literature recommended using Plasticine to render rooms gas-proof by plugging up keyholes and sealing door and window surrounds. It is also likely that the material was used, as it was originally

(continued on p. 72)

WOMEN AND BATH'S WAR EFFORT

The emancipation of women that was much accelerated during the First World War gathered momentum during the Second. Although conscription was not extended to women until 1941, volunteers were encouraged to 'do their bit' from the early part of the war. Among the earliest were recruits to Civil Defence, and 62-year-old Mrs Florence Davis was noted by the *Chronicle* in May 1940 'as a good example'. She was attached to H12 ARP Group at Green Park, the preparedness of which would be severely tested during the Bath blitz two years later.

As in the First World War, women of eighteen and over were soon working on Bath Tramways Company's buses as conductresses. Among them was Mrs E.W. Hooper, who was an old hand at clipping tickets having taken fares on the Bath trams during the previous war. By the summer of 1940 fifteen women were serving on the city's buses where, for a 48-hour week, they were paid a wage of between £2 4s and £2 12s 1d, according to age; after six months' service this might rise to a maximum of £2 19s 3d. By Christmas 1941 women were also driving buses. Miss Millicent Young of Penn Hill, Weston, was one of the first women to drive a public service vehicle in the city and the *Chronicle* reported that 'she is also au fait with the mechanical side'.

The shortage of manpower was becoming acute and special appeals were made by the Mayor for women volunteers to serve in a long list of non-combatant organisations that included the ARP, Auxiliary Fire Service, Civil Nursing Reserve, British Red Cross Society, WVS, Women's Land Army, Blood Transfusion Service, the Army and LDV. In June 1941 Bath's Ministry of Information Committee held a big recruitment drive to encourage women to join the forces and war factories and backed it up with a huge parade of women's services. But voluntary appeals were proving unsuccessful and in December 1941 the call-up was extended to unmarried women and widows between the ages of twenty and thirty. In Bath it was estimated that between 600 and 700 women would register for National Service on Saturday 6 December. The recruitment of women for the armed forces and war work continued throughout the war, with the campaign being kept alive locally by photographs and articles in the *Chronicle* showing Bath women 'doing a fine job for the war effort'.

In the meantime, women porters were working alongside men at the GWR goods station, loading and unloading wagons and lorries. The *Chronicle* noted that 'They like their wartime job – and the men like them!'. Members of the Co-operative Women's Guild entertained soldiers convalescing in local hospitals and the WVS was active in demonstrating schemes for setting up house in 48 hours following an air raid. WVS members also volunteered to serve as drivers and attendants on the two Ford food vans (see p. 61). To help warn of impending attack from the air, women also became watchers of the skies, manning local Observer Corps posts in and around the city. They also volunteered for the important job of Civil Defence fire watchers.

At Christmastide women volunteers from local churches worked feverishly in church halls, packing parcels of food and small gifts for despatch to members of Britain's armed forces serving overseas. Housewives were encouraged to set up street savings groups under the watchful eye of the National Savings Movement.

Upper Weston women preparing an air raid shelter.

Miss Millicent Young was one of Bath's first women bus drivers.

In Walcot Street, Bath Soroptimists ran a Women's Services Club with the slogan 'Come right in'.

During the war years, several Bath women were appointed to roles within the city that for many years had been the traditional domain of men. Of the five newly appointed magistrates for the city in 1942, it was noteworthy that two were women: Mrs Robert Pitt and Miss Kathleen Harper, both of whom served in this capacity for many years. Women also began to serve as sidesmen in parish churches since there appeared to be no legal obstacle to their appointment. The Parochial Church Council (Powers) Measure expressly provided that 'all persons who are on the electoral role shall be eligible for office'.

The Second World War advanced the cause of female emancipation in Britain significantly, but women still had to shout to make their voices heard in what remained a largely male-dominated society. However, the huge contribution made by women to the war effort was indisputable and in time would lead to greater equality for them in the workplace.

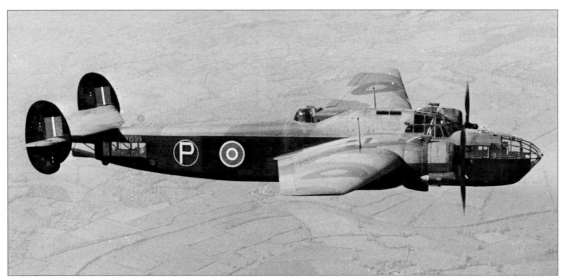

Wooden components for the Armstrong Whitworth Albemarle were made at Bath Cabinet Makers on the Lower Bristol Road. (Authors)

Plasticine was invented by William Harbutt in 1897 and manufactured at Bathampton. It is suggested in this advertisement that Plasticine, a unique modelling material, can be pressed into war service by helping to make homes safe in the event of poison gas attacks. (Bath Industrial Heritage Centre)

intended, as a modelling material – but this time by specialist model makers at the top secret Allied Central Interpretation Unit at Medmenham in Buckinghamshire. Here, with the help of photographs taken by RAF and US Army Air Force photo-reconnaissance aircraft, accurate scale models were built of key enemy targets, such as the Ruhr dams in Germany and the Gestapo headquarters in Copenhagen, where precision bombing attacks were crucial. Allied bomber crews could view a three-dimensional model of their intended target and its surroundings at pre-raid briefings, allowing them to memorise important landmarks and topographical features that would help them locate the target.

Smaller industrial enterprises in Bath with a direct link to the war effort were the British Overseas Airways Corporation (BOAC) repair facilities located at Bath Garages in James Street West and at Isaac Pitman's in the Lower Bristol Road, both of which were used for the overhaul of aircraft propellers. BOAC's main base in the West Country was at Whitchurch airport near Bristol.

CHAPTER 9
Crime and Punishment

For many of us today, the Britain of the Second World War seems a place peopled with heroes and one in which ordinary men and women pulled together for the common good. It was a nation where children were well behaved – seen and not heard – and where everyone put their own selfish ambitions to one side and worked towards beating Nazi Germany. But the reality could be very different.

It is recorded that, in 1939, a little over 300,000 indictable offences were known to the police in England and Wales. Alarmingly, by 1943 this figure had risen to 370,000 and it continued to climb to a peak of 478,000 in 1945. However, it is reassuring to note that convictions for crimes of violence against the person had risen very little, and the number of people found guilty of non-indictable offences had actually dropped from almost 500,000 in 1939 to 280,000 in 1943. Much of this was attributed to the petrol shortage – traffic offences and resultant prosecutions plummeted. New classes of offences had been created with the outbreak of war, those against Defence Regulations, of which black-out infringements were the most numerous: 300,000 in 1940, the peak year.

Bath was no exception to these national trends and in fact the myth of the sedate spa city, where elderly maiden aunts went to take the waters and blimpish colonels propped up the lounge bar in the Grand Pump Room Hotel, conceals the real story. The city suffered its share of theft, assault, child abuse, juvenile crime, 'joy riding' and anti-social behaviour, as the pages of the *Chronicle* for the war years illustrate with amazing regularity.

'PUT THAT B—— LIGHT OUT!' CRIMES AGAINST DEFENCE REGULATIONS

Under the new Defence Regulations, motorists were warned in January 1940 that it would be illegal to use any type of headlight mask other than the officially approved model, and before the month was out the first cases for lights offences were heard by the city's magistrates – but these involved cyclists whose lights did not comply with the Lighting Restrictions Order. Hand-held torches were in big demand to guide pedestrians around the blacked-out streets of Bath, and in March fines were imposed on people who flashed 'unscreened' hand torches. It was also alleged that some city shop keepers were profiteering on batteries for these torches, and the public was invited to report those retailers whom they thought were guilty of overcharging.

The warden's familiar cry of 'Put that b—— light out!' was frequently heard, the guilty offenders being summoned for 'failing to obscure lights'. Reports such as the following are typical: 'For causing a light to be displayed at St Peter's Terrace at 5.35 p.m., Edward Jefferies was fined 5*s* by Bath magistrates this morning. For a similar offence at 6.15 p.m., Iris Davies of Bennett Street was also fined 5*s*.'

In what the *Chronicle* described as 'one of the worst Bath cases', John Watts of 8 Queen's place, Widcombe, was sentenced to seven days' imprisonment for a black-out offence on 22 October 1943. A custodial sentence for a black-out offence was very unusual.

Minor offences such as these were common and dealt with by magistrates on a regular basis during the early years of the war. Bath firms were also within reach of the long arm of Defence Regulations. In January 1941 the police visited the premises of J. Lyons & Co., the caterers, in Union Street, where more than thirty people were employed. The firm was fined £1 for 'failing to secure that a person who had undertaken to act as a fire watcher was at all times present'. In June that year, five employees of a different Bath firm were each fined £3 for failing to take turns fire watching in April and May.

On 29 April 1944 the first case in Bath for failing to take reasonable care to preserve a Morrison shelter was heard at Bath Police Court. The City Engineer's Department regularly inspected and noted the conditions of these shelters and warned householders that 'if any more cases of misuse are discovered there will be corresponding prosecutions'.

Unfortunately, the black-out seemed to encourage some of the more malodorous characteristics of human behaviour to come to the fore, as the *Chronicle* of 5 April 1940 reported:

Got to be Stopped: Black-out Shopdoor Nuisance at Bath
The practice of using shop doorways as public conveniences was strongly criticised by magistrates at the Bath City Police Court this morning. 'It is very disgusting and this has got to be stopped' declared the chairman Mrs Devenish. Det-Insp. Coles said that the Chief Constable had asked him to point out that the offence is becoming a terrible nuisance. The clerk (Mr W.E. Lisle Bentham) said that six summonses for such offences were issued by him on Thursday.

LOOTING

One of the most serious criminal offences in Britain during the war was looting from bombed-out houses or business premises. Punishment for this offence was severe – penal servitude for life if your case was heard by an understanding judge, and the gallows if not. If allowed to go unchecked, looting could become a major problem to the maintenance of law and order in any town or city where bomb damage to property had occurred and peoples' belongings and shop goods were scattered in the debris. In the wake of the Bath blitz, the city was lucky in that it didn't suffer the same high level of looting experienced in some other British cities of the time, but nevertheless a number of cases were reported in the *Chronicle*.

In the immediate aftermath of the blitz, the city police reported that looting had been negligible, but reports of several instances, and one of a looter apparently being shot dead by the Home Guard, found their way into the paper. The *Chronicle* of 4 May 1942 reported:

When the question of looting was raised at the Bath Emergency Committee's meeting this morning the Chief Constable Mr H.P. Hind said that there might be a little in the early stages; he was unable to say that there had been none.

Colonel Guy Rogers of the Home Guard told the committee that when a report came in that there was a tendency to loot in a certain area, with the Chief Constable's agreement he put on a picket to control the district to keep people out.

'Complaints of looting have been negligible' was the authoritative statement made by the Chief Constable this morning.

Bomb-damaged shops on Wellsway. With their goods scattered in the road, premises such as these were easy prey for looters.

   Home Guards with live ammunition in their rifles patrolled the streets, it had been stated. When on patrol duty, however, they always carry live ammunition. Despite a rumour, there has been no shooting and the story being circulated that a man was shot dead by the Home Guard is described as 'nonsense'.

Throughout May, reports of looters coming before the Bench appeared in the columns of the *Chronicle*. This brief report appeared on 7 May 1942:

   A case of alleged looting in Bath came before Bath City magistrates on Saturday when there was a weeks remand in custody. Accused was Eric Blakemore, a soldier, and he was charged with stealing from premises recently damaged by enemy action two rings, the property of some person, or persons unknown, on April 29th.

And on 24 August:

Caught With Loot
Articles from blitzed house. Six months for charge hand
He had been engaged on demolition work in Bath. When he reached Paddington with two large packages he aroused the interest of police officers. On investigation they discovered a variety of articles which it was subsequently found had been removed from blitzed houses in Oldfield Park. As a result Thomas Pitcher, 41, of Hackney, appeared at Bath Police Court. He was sentenced to six months imprisonment.

A government official, inspecting the damage at Bath, turned to commiserate with a man searching feverishly among the debris of what had been his home.

'Can I help you?' he asked. 'No' was the reply. 'When I find the blackguard who has stolen my watering can, I'm going to knock his head off.'

RAPE

Instances of rape in wartime Bath were virtually unheard of. But on 29 May 1944 the *Chronicle* carried a report of the death sentence being passed on a black American GI for an attack on a Combe Down woman. At a Court Martial hearing, evidence was given that Corporal T/5 Leroy Henry, aged thirty, had knocked one night on the door of a lorry driver's cottage at Combe Down to ask the way. The lorry driver's wife looked out of the window and told him, but he seemed uncertain and asked her to write the directions down for him. Instead, she dressed hastily and went out to see him on his way. After the alleged incident, she said, she met her husband as she was running home and persuaded him from chasing the accused because he had a knife. Henry was found guilty of rape and sentenced to be hanged.

There was obviously more to this case than met the eye for it appeared very much that Henry had been convicted on the flimsiest of evidence. The *Chronicle* of 5 June recorded that Bathonians had taken up the case of Leroy Henry with huge fervour. Alderman Day (Labour) gave much of his time to the organisation of a direct appeal for clemency to General Eisenhower and a petition signed by 33,000 Bathonians was duly forwarded to him for consideration. On 22 June it was reported in the *Chronicle* that 'HQ European Theater of Operations US Army announces that Cpl T/5 Leroy Henry whose sentence of death for alleged rape was disapproved by General Dwight D. Eisenhower, has returned to duty'.

CHILD NEGLECT AND ABUSE

Sadly, child neglect and abuse carry on regardless of momentous world-shaping events – including world wars. This 'very sordid story' was reported in the *Chronicle* during April 1940. The full name and address of the defendant appeared in the original – and much fuller – report, but the present authors have omitted these details to prevent any embarrassment to the children referred to in the article:

Month's Hard Labour for Father

'We have listened with great pain to this very sordid story. It is difficult to understand how parents of any class can see their children living under such conditions as these – horrible conditions,' observed Mr Rhodes Cork who, sitting with Mr R.N. Green-Armytage at Bath Police Court this morning, sentenced William ——, of —— Street, to a month's hard labour for ill-treating and neglecting his children in a manner likely to cause them unnecessary suffering or injury to their health. . . . Both he and Mrs —— denied ill-treating their children and said the evidence was exaggerated.

'BOYS (AND GIRLS) WILL BE BOYS'
JUVENILE CRIME AND DELINQUENCY

Juvenile crime and delinquency might be considered as a phenomenon of the late twentieth century, but in wartime Bath it was clearly a big headache for both the police and youth organisations. Citizens were appalled at what the youth of the

city got up to during the black-out and for some time there had been concern about young people idling away the hours on the streets at night. In January 1941 an appeal was made to the public for information about hooligans who had thrown life-buoys into the River Avon. Worse was to come; in May five youths, aged between seventeen and twenty, hit a police sergeant on the head with his own helmet in 'a savage assault' during the black-out. They were all sent to prison.

Under-age drinking was a problem and it was suggested that additional policewomen were needed to join in more regular patrols of the public parks and gardens, and that the identity cards of young people frequenting public houses in the city should be checked occasionally. The concerns of a local vigilante association, which went as far as asking for a curfew to be placed on girls aged fifteen and under, were borne out in July 1944 when a fourteen-year-old Bath girl (deemed uncontrollable at previous court hearings) was sent to an approved school on account of her liaisons with American soldiers in a park at midnight.

The city's parks were not only the preferred rendezvous for young girls and sex-starved soldiers looking for a good time, but also the playground of vandals and hooligans. In July 1941 three boys – two of them evacuees from London – were charged with breaking twenty-five panes of glass valued at £3 10s at a shed in Hedgemead Park:

'Hooligans in Bath parks were being treated too leniently', a Bath Alderman told the Parks Committee. 'Older lads throw water about; their language and customs are appalling, and one of them threw dirt at a lady.' The chairman said, 'I think the schoolteachers should do something. These children go away from school and collect in the parks and do all the damage they can.'

Sometimes the war could have direct and unavoidable affects on proceedings, as a report in the *Chronicle* of 1 May 1942 (four days after the city had been rocked by heavy bombing) revealed:

Accused and Witnesses Missing: Bath Summonses Adjourned

Of six boys who should have appeared in Bath Juvenile Court on Thursday in connection with damage to the extent of £14 to a public toilet and an air-raid shelter, both in Hedgemead Park, only three were present. It transpired that some of the boys lived in houses which had suffered by the recent raids; that houses, to say nothing of the boys, could not be found; that one boy was injured, and that witnesses were missing. In the circumstances it was deemed impossible to proceed and the hearing was adjourned for a month.

It may be surprising to learn too that, according to a report from the *Chronicle* of 22 April 1940, car theft and 'joy riding' by youths is not the preserve of the 1990s:

Camden Crescent Drama
Narrow Escape for Pursuing Bath Police – Youths in Court

The allegation that three Bath youths in a stolen car alighted at the top of a steep rise and released the brakes which made the car run backwards out of control in the path of a pursuing police car, was made at Bath this morning, when John Patridge (18), William Thompson (19) of the Bath Lads' Home,

7 Norfolk Crescent, and a boy of 15, were charged with stealing a Morris 10hp car, valued at £150, the property of Charles Geoffrey Moss.

The Inspector said that on Sunday a car was taken from Park Lane. PC Simmonds and PWR Haste were later patrolling Lansdown Road in a police car. They were going up the road and they saw the stolen car coming down. They turned round and followed. The stolen car went along Camden Crescent. As the police car entered the crescent, the defendants alighted from the other car at the top of the steep rise leading to the crescent and, it was alleged, released the brakes. The three youths were remanded in custody accordingly, and other matters will be investigated in the meantime.

'TROUSERS TOO WIDE'
ENFORCING FOOD AND CLOTHING RESTRICTIONS

With foodstuffs and clothing in short supply and virtually every commodity available only on ration, the authorities were naturally concerned that nothing was wasted. They were also vigilant in the enforcement of rationing regulations. In September 1941 the first prosecution for wasting food was heard in Bath when a woman from Shakespeare Avenue was fined for placing four loaves, 'hard, stale and mouldy', on top of a pig bin. The following month the *Chronicle* reported that a Bath tradesman, Harry B. Dawes, tailor and outfitter, was fined 5s 'for selling clothes and shoes, rationed goods, without receiving from the customer the appropriate number of coupons'.

The rag trade came under further scrutiny in 1943 when the *Chronicle* of 15 June reported the city's first tailoring restrictions case:

Contemptuous Penalty – and No Costs

That suits had been made with too many pockets in jackets, back straps to waistcoats, pleats to trousers, and trousers too wide, were some of the allegations against a well-known Bath tailor, Albert Edward Fry, of Union Passage, when he was prosecuted by the Board of Trade for eleven alleged offences against the Restrictions specified in the Schedule to the Making of Civilian Clothing (Restrictions) Order, 1942.

Eventually restrictions were eased and on 25 January 1944 it was reported that:

. . . now everyone wants 'turn-ups' in suits. Customers who have suits on order overwhelmed Bath tailors today by inquiries whether they will take advantage of the relaxation in 'austerity styles', whereby turn-ups and a full array of pockets in men's suits are to return, with double-breasted jackets if desired.

'CAN I DO YOU NOW, SIR?' – THE OLDEST PROFESSION

Bath police had been keeping their eye on a certain house in Thomas Street, London Road, since early in the war, following a tip-off from a nosy neighbour. Servicemen had been seen entering and leaving the house on a number of occasions and upon investigation the police found that the house was being used as a brothel.

CHAPTER 10

All Work and No Play

RECREATION IN WARTIME BATH

There may have been a war on, but people from every town and city across Britain needed to forget the harsh reality every now and again, and the citizens of Bath were no exception. The opportunity to escape into the glamorous world of the silver screen – albeit it in a fuggy crowded cinema – or to foxtrot the night away at a dance hall – if only with fellow members of the local Home Guard and their wives – provided the temporary release craved by many from the privations of the war years. Cinema-going, dances and the theatre, not forgetting the home entertainment of those years, the wonderful wireless, all helped achieve this end.

Wireless

Entertainment for the majority meant an evening spent at home, drawing the heavy black-out curtains and huddling round the family wireless set to listen to the voice of the BBC. Programmes were transmitted on three stations. The authoritative Home Service carried the all-important news bulletins and programmes of a fairly serious nature. The news-readers were Alvar Liddell and John Snagge and those who remember wartime news bulletins will not forget the familiar announcement: 'This is the BBC Home Service. Here is the news and this is Alvar Liddell reading it.'

The Light Programme, as its name implies, carried programmes of a lighter nature. And there was the Forces Programme, which began broadcasting a daily twelve hours of light entertainment for the troops in 1940. Curiously enough, 'The Brains Trust' with the philosopher Professor C.E.M. Joad, the scientist Dr Julian Huxley, and a retired naval officer Commander A.B. Campbell, was created specially for the Forces Programme and became very popular with its listeners, military and civilian alike. Although strictly against regulations, it was not unheard of for wireless operators in RAF bomber aircraft returning from a raid to tune their receivers to the Forces Programme so all the crew could listen in.

Among the many popular wartime songs that caught on in a big way were those of British No. 1 Forces' Sweetheart Vera Lynn, whose half-hour radio programme 'Sincerely Yours' was broadcast on the Forces Programme. 'The White Cliffs of Dover', 'We'll Meet Again' and 'A Nightingale Sang in Berkeley Square' are among her most famous numbers. Ironically, it was a German song, 'Lili Marleen', overheard by certain troops of the British 8th Army during the North African Campaign, that became one of the biggest hits of the war in its English version, 'Lili Marlene – My Lili of the Lamplight'. It even equalled the First World War's 'It's a Long Way to Tipperary', but the Ministry of Information was unable to commission a song to rival its popularity.

Other well-remembered programmes from the war years include Tommy Handley's comedy series 'ITMA' ('It's That Man Again') with its mixture of catch-phrases, funny characters and irreverent humour, 'Music While You Work',

14

THURSDAY Home Service

JUNE 4

203.5 m. 1474 kc/s   391.1 m. 767 kc/s
449.1 m. 668 kc/s   49.34 m. 6.08 Mc/s

BLACK-OUT STARTS—
London 10.54   Plymouth 11.5
Cardiff 11.7   Leeds 11.14
Edinburgh 11.49 Aberdeen 11.54

7.0 a.m. Time, Big Ben : **NEWS**
and summary of today's programmes
for the Forces

7.15   MORNING STAR
Records of Alexander Kipnis (bass)

**7.30   'UP IN THE MORNING
EARLY'**
Exercises for men : Coleman Smith
7.40 Exercises for women : Audrey
Nicol

7.50   TUNE FOR TODAY
An anthology of favourites

7.55   'LIFT UP YOUR HEARTS'
Short morning prayers

8.0   Time, Greenwich : NEWS
Programme Parade

8.15   THE KITCHEN FRONT
'A Man in the Kitchen'

8.20   'TAKE YOUR CHOICE'
Records taken at random from the
rack

9.0   JACK WILSON
and his Versatile Five, with Mary
Pollock (soprano)
Meet the Boys..............arr. Jack Wilson
Songs :
The Stars..........Montague Phillips
June..........................Quilter
Gypsy Song and Czardas..........Carlos
Rose of Tralee..............arr. Kane
Songs :
Today is ours..............Eric Coates
Oh, tell me, nightingale....Lisa Lehmann
Speakeasy..........................Gensler
Jackpot..............................Gaida
Song : Neglected Moon...Armstrong Gibbs
Crown and Anchor..............Whittam
Piano Medley

'LIBERTYMEN

FALL IN!'

You can spend another half-hour
with your friends of the ship's
company tonight at 10.30

Song : The cherry tree doth bloom
Red Resin..........................Goatley
Red Resin..........................Hellier
Honeysuckle Rose..................Waller

9.45   REGINALD NEW
at the organ of the Regal, Beckenham

10.5   FOR THE SCHOOLS
News commentary and interlude

10.15   Time, Greenwich
THE DAILY SERVICE
from p. 21 of 'New Every Morning'
and p. 48 of 'Each Returning Day'

10.30 MUSIC WHILE YOU WORK
Rhythmic records

11.0   FOR THE SCHOOLS
11.0 THE MUSICAL TRAVELLER : The
Traveller's son finds that his voice is
changing.   His father tells him what
may happen to it, and describes the
various kinds of human voice and
how they are used in music
11.20 INTERMEDIATE FRENCH : by
Jean-Jacques Oberlin, Yvonne Oberlin, and Marie Touchard. Concours :
'Allo ! Allo ! ' Les élèves auront à
deviner quelle est la personne qui
parle au téléphone, et de quoi elle
parle
11.40 SENIOR GEOGRAPHY ; Making
the Americas : Latin , America.
'Sheep in Patagonia and Tierra del
Fuego', by James Douglas

P.M.

12.0 BBC SALON ORCHESTRA
Conductor, Leslie Bridgewater
Mascarade..........................Sullivan
The way you look tonight..........Kern
The Skaters' Waltz............Waldteufel
Humoreske........................Dvořák
Canny Cummerlan'......Gerrard Williams
Serenade at Sunset..........Haydn Wood
Masque, As You Like It : Woodland
Dance—Children's Dance—Rustic Dance
Edward German

12.30 WORKERS' PLAYTIME
Lunch-time entertainment for fac-
tory-workers, from a factory somewhere in Britain. (Recorded)

1.0   Time, Greenwich : NEWS

1.15 CALLING ALL WOMEN
'Calling the Home Front' : talk by
Naomi Jacob

1.20   MAURICE WINNICK
and his Band

2.0   FOR THE SCHOOLS
2.0 NATURE STUDY : 'Lobsters', by
A. J. Mee
2.15   Interval music
2.20 PHYSICAL TRAINING : (for use
in classrooms) by Edith Dowling
2.35   Interval music
2.40 SENIOR HISTORY : 1850-1942.
Learning to know the Empire :
'Stories from our history that I
learnt at school'. 1—By a Canadian,
Stanley Maxted

2.0 MUSIC WHILE YOU WORK
Primo Scala's Accordion Band, under
the direction of Harry Bidgood

**3.30   BBC
NORTHERN ORCHESTRA**
Conducted by Warwick Braithwaite
Overture : The Hebrides......Mendelssohn
Symphony No. 55, in E flat (The School-
master)..............................Haydn
Ballet Suite No. 1..................Gluck

4.15 THE FORTNIGHT'S FILMS
Colin Wills

4.30   IVY BENSON
and her Ladies Dance Orchestra

5.0   Newyddion (News in Welsh)

5.5 GWASANAETH GOSBER
(Studio Service in Welsh). Cymerir y
Gweddïau o'r llyfr 'Bob Bore o
Newydd'

5.20   CHILDREN'S HOUR
5.20 Visit to the Clifton Zoo, conducted by Mac
5.45 Talk on Gardening, by D.
Manning.

6.0   Time, Greenwich : NEWS
National and Regional announcements

6.30   'BLACK GALLERY'
4—'Himmler'. Written by John
Dickson-Carr. Produced by Walter
Rilla. (Recording of this programme
will be broadcast in the Forces programme on Saturday at 1.15 p.m.)

6.45   SANDY MACPHERSON
at the theatre organ

7.0   'COLLECTORS' CORNER'
Second of a series of gramophone
programmes presented by Compton
Mackenzie

7.10   'COUNTRY EXPERIENCE'
A talk

7.20   FARM RECORD

7.30   News in Norwegian

7.45   HILDEGARDE
The intimate singer, on gramophone
records

**8.0   LONDON
SUMMER CONCERTS**
Under the auspices of Allied Govern-
ments. Organised by the Royal Phil-
harmonic Society. Sixth concert :
BBC Symphony Orchestra (leader,
Paul Beard), conducted by Sir
Henry Wood
Symphony No. 7 (Leningrad)
Shostakovich
First performance in England
From the Royal Albert Hall, London
(See Ralph Hill's article on page 4)

9.0   Time, Big Ben : NEWS

9.25   WAR COMMENTARY

SIR HENRY WOOD
conducts the Leningrad Symphony
by Shostakovich in the broadcast
from the London Summer Concerts
at the Royal Albert Hall tonight
at 8.0.

9.40   'MARCHING ON'
General editor, Robert Barr. Produced by John Glyn-Jones
Every week the news brings from a world-
wide battle-front fresh stories of courage,
endurance, humour, and heroism. These
topical feature programmes re-tell them
in radio form, dramatising the forward
march of the peoples of the United
Nations.

**10.10   SHORT
MID-WEEK SERVICE**
Address by the Rev. Derrick Greeves

10.30 'LIBERTYMEN, FALL IN !'
Another thirty minutes with the
ship's company. Music by
Leading Writer Roland Blackburn.
Music by Signalman Geoffrey
Wright. Radio adaptation by David
Yates-Mason. Produced by Reginald
Smith
Master-at-Arms........Roderick Jones
Tom..................Reginald Purdell
Bill....................John Carol
Stripey................Dick Francis
Shorty................Harold Scott
The Commander.......Horace Percival
The Captain..........Ewart Scott
Dorothy.............Helen Raymond
Fanny..............Marjorie Westbury
Young Tommy........Ronnie Beadle
His mother............Kitty de Legh
Male Chorus and augmented BBC
Revue Orchestra, conducted by
Hyam Greenbaum
(Special BBC recording of the broad-
cast on December 8, 1941)

11.0   RUSSIAN SONGS
sung by Oda Slobodskaya
On the Hills of Georgia ; The Nymph ;
Spring................Rimsky-Korsakov
The Magpie : Two Songs from Songs
of the Nursery : In the Corner ;
Prayer at Bedtime..............Mussorgsky

11.15 'THE WONDERFUL DOG'
Short story, written by the Russian
humorist Zoshchenko, and read by
G. R. Schjelderup

11.20 MAURICE WINNICK
and his Band

12.0 midnight-12.20 a.m.
Time, Greenwich : NEWS

A page from the Radio Times *in 1942. Among the popular programmes on the Home Service
were 'Music While You Work' and 'Workers Playtime', which preceded the One O'Clock News.
The forces programme broadcast shows such as 'Break for Music' – concerts performed by
members of ENSA – 'Ack-Ack, Beer-Beer' – a twice weekly radio magazine for men and
women in Anti-Aircraft and Balloon Barrage units – and 'The Brains Trust'. (Authors)*

'Workers' Playtime' with its catchy signature tune, and 'Children's Hour' with Derek McCulloch. It was also possible to tune in to German Radio's English language broadcast and listen to – and occasionally laugh at – the propaganda of 'Lord Haw-Haw' (William Joyce), which he always opened with the same phrase 'Jarminy calling, Jarminy calling . . .'. An American-Irish-Briton, Joyce was a former supporter of the British Fascist leader Oswald Moseley, whose broadcasts aimed to undermine British confidence in the news supplied by the heavily censored wartime press. Curiosity and the lack of interesting war news gained 'Lord Haw-Haw' a big audience in Britain.

Cinema

At the outbreak of war all cinemas across Britain were ordered to close until further notice, the authorities fearing massive loss of life if bombs hit public places crowded with people. But the long-awaited Nazi bombing of England did not materialise immediately and within a few weeks the panic subsided and cinema opening began to return to normal, although it was not until February 1941 that cinemas in Bath were allowed to open on Sundays.

Cinema-going became hugely popular. In fact across the whole of Britain at this time some 25 to 30 million cinema tickets were sold every week. People queued for hours to see the latest films screened at the Beau Nash in Westgate Street, the Odeon and the Forum in Southgate, the Little Theatre in St Michael's Place, and the Scala at Oldfield Park.

As a tragic aside, when the Scala publicised its programme for Saturday 25 April 1942 in the *Chronicle*, included in the advertisement was the reassurance of 'Safety First Air Raid Shelter, opposite Cinema'. In the heavy bombing that was unleashed on the city that very night, this shelter received a direct hit from a bomb and was completely destroyed, killing more than twenty people who had sought refuge there.

The classic *Gone With the Wind* (1939) became one of the greatest films to be screened during the war years, running continuously in London's West End from 1940 to 1944 and much enjoyed by cinema audiences in Bath too. Other box-office hits included:

Wartime advertisements in the Chronicle *during June 1941 for a play at the Theatre Royal, light entertainment at the nearby Palace Theatre, and Bath cinema programmes including* The Ghost Train *by Bath's own playwright Arnold Ridley, who is best known for his role as 'Private Godfrey' in the BBC's ever-popular* Dad's Army.

Noel Coward's patriotic stiff upper-lip film about the Navy, *In Which We Serve* (1942); *The Gentle Sex* (1943), which portrayed the role women were playing in Britain's war effort; Laurence Olivier's equally patriotic Shakespearean epic *Henry V* (1944), with its exciting footage of the Battle of Agincourt; and another of Coward's wartime successes *Brief Encounter* (1945), starring Celia Johnson and Trevor Howard.

Among many other films seen by Bath cinema audiences was the classic *Phantom of the Opera*– terror in glorious Technicolor – with Nelson Eddy, Susanna Foster and Claude Rains; Margaret Lockwood, James Mason and Phyllis Calvert starred in *The Man in Grey*; another favourite was *Prisoner of Zenda*, with Ronald Coleman and Madeleine Carroll. In the last year of the war city cinema-goers were able to see Tommy Trinder and Stanley Holloway in *Champagne Charlie is in Town* and George Formby in *She Snoops to Conquer*. How many, too, can remember Merle Oberon in the romantic *A Song to Remember*, which was also screened at Bath during the last year of the war?

Theatre

Bath's two theatres, situated facing each other across the Sawclose, entertained audiences throughout the war. During Bath & District 'War Weapons Week' in February 1941 Jean Forbes Robertson, supported by a West End cast, performed *Berkeley Square* at the Theatre Royal, while across the road a full variety programme was billed at the Palace Theatre. In 1943 lovers of light music could buy tickets at the Theatre Royal to see the greatest of all musical plays *The Desert Song*, with Arthur Lucas, Doris Francis and Wilfred Watson – all very well known in their day – and a full supporting company of principals, chorus and orchestra. At the time of the D-Day landings in June 1944, Terence Rattigan's acclaimed play about the RAF, *Flarepath*, was being staged at the Theatre Royal after a successful eighteen-month run at London's Apollo Theatre. In April the following year devotees of Noel Coward could see his play *This Happy Breed*.

Across the Sawclose at the Palace Theatre in 1944, Rex Stewart Productions presented a new nautical review *Salute the Navy* – '16 salvos of continuous laughter' – and in the same year Anglo–American Productions staged the 'all-star road show' *Stage Door*, featuring the delectable Jane of the *Daily Mirror*. 'Millions of you have been amused by her cartoons – now meet her personally!' proclaimed the advertisement for the show. In January 1945 the Palace had visits from Felix Mendelssohn and his Hawaiian Serenaders supported by the popular comedian Stainless Steven – billed as 'brilliant comedy' – and two months later 'Radio's Queen of Comedy' Suzette Tari. In April 1945 came the review appropriately entitled *In Civvies Again!*

Concerts

During the war years Bath was fortunate to be visited by a stream of internationally famous performers – and many who were not so famous – to entertain its audiences. After the war many became household names, such as Sir Thomas Beecham and Sir John Barbirolli. Throughout the war the city authorities continued to support an orchestra, the Bath Philharmonic, which was under the direction of A. Ernest Monk who, in an impassioned appeal in the *Chronicle* for a concert hall, pleaded 'Make our lovely city an English Salzburg'. To war-weary Bathonians, the reference to Austria

– Hitler's native land – might not have been so well received. The Pavilion (referred to as a 'barn of a building' by the famous orchestral conductor Sir Thomas Beecham) was used for most concerts, recitals and popular dances.

A proposal to use Bath Abbey for a concert by Bath Philharmonic in October 1943 provoked a letter of outraged indignation from a resident who regarded such an act as 'tantamount to the commercialising' of the church. A letter of reply to the exasperated Bath resident was published in the *Chronicle* of 23 October, signed mysteriously by 'One of the Orchestra':

> No doubt the gentleman who wrote to you criticising the project was well intentioned, but his judgement of the matter is obviously hasty, and it is very unfair in more than one respect. The main feature of the afternoon's music is to be an organ concerto by a composer whose name is little known generally [Rheinberger] . . . I venture to say that the concerto that is to be played is unknown to most people . . . and it will be Bath's privilege to hear this work played by one of the greatest organists of our time. Where then would your critic suggest such glorious music be heard? In the Pavilion? There is no organ! And if there were! In the city hall? Where is it to be found? It is then fitting and right that on such an occasion Bath should turn to the mother of music, the church. That music should be rendered in our glorious and beautiful Abbey for there is the organ and the atmosphere. . .

BATH BATH
EVENTS FOR February, 1941   EVENTS FOR February, 1941

EVERY SUNDAY.
   THE ABBEY—8 a.m., 11 a.m. and 3.30 p.m.
   PAVILION—7 SPECIAL CONCERT.

EVERY TUESDAY.
   PAVILION—7.30 to 9.30 POPULAR DANCE. Arthur Clark and his Band.
   Eastern Dispensary.—3.0. Whist Drive.

EVERY WEDNESDAY.
   Old Post Office.—7.30 "Friendship" Whist Drive in aid of Local Hospitals.

EVERY THURSDAY.
   Pump Room.—3.0 P.D.S.A. Whist Drive.
   St. Barnabas' Church Room, Southdown.—7.30. W.E.A. Lectures, " International Relations, 1919–1939." Mr. A. Percival, B.A.
   Forum. 4 to 6.45. Tea Dance.

EVERY FRIDAY.
   Pavilion.—7.30 to 9.30. POPULAR DANCE. Arthur Clark and his Band.

EVERY SATURDAY.
   PUMP ROOM—7 to 9.45 DANCE. Reg. Ball and his Band. Two Floors, Two Bands.
   ASSEMBLY ROOMS—7.30 to 10.30 BUFFET DANCE. Refreshments at Licensed Buffet. Uniform or Evening Dress. Arthur Clark & his Band.
   Old Post Office.—7.30 " Friendship" Whist Drive in aid of Local Hospitals.
   Forum. 4 to 6.45. Tea Dance.

ISSUED BY THE CITY OF BATH INFORMATION BUREAU.
Here Visitors may obtain information free on all matters of interest.
Open 9 to 1, 2.30 to 6.
Communications should be addressed to John Hatton, Spa Director, Bath. Tel. 4227.

As they still do today, Bath Information Bureau issued a monthly leaflet during the war years detailing events of all kinds in the city. (Authors)

Among the musical attractions offered in autumn 1944 was a return visit to the city by a pianist called Louis Godowsky (not to be confused with the famous Leopold Godowsky). Louis was said to have appeared in Bath as a child with the pianist Solomon, and later as a soloist in concertos with the Pump Room Orchestra. In the same year, 1944, the Halle Orchestra, under its distinguished conductor John Barbirolli, paid its first visit to the city, and the following month the City of Birmingham Orchestra, under its conductor George Weldon, gave a concert in the Pavilion with Moura Lympany as soloist in Greig's Piano Concerto. The CBO returned again in January 1945, this time with soloists Irene Kohler and Benno Moiseiwitsch. The Philharmonic Orchestra, under its Austrian-born British conductor Karl Rankl, appeared at the Pavilion in February. Early in 1945 the 77-year-old Scottish pianist Frederick Lamond gave a Beethoven recital at the Pump Room, and some time later another Beethoven recital was given by the Bristol pianist Eric Hodges, a frequent recitalist at Bath after the war. Pianist Myra Hess (London-born and English despite her name), whose lunch-time concerts at the London National Gallery attracted capacity audiences, played at Bath in March 1945, and in the following month Solomon, another frequent visitor to the city, gave a recital at the Pavilion.

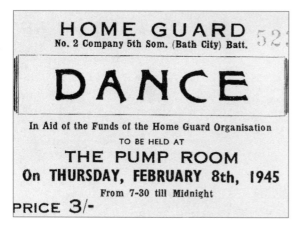

HOME GUARD
No. 2 Company 5th Som. (Bath City) Batt.

DANCE

In Aid of the Funds of the Home Guard Organisation
TO BE HELD AT

THE PUMP ROOM

On THURSDAY, FEBRUARY 8th, 1945
From 7-30 till Midnight

PRICE 3/-

During wartime, dances brought together people from all walks of life, and profits were usually donated to worthy causes. This ticket was for a dance in 1945 promoted by No. 2 Company 5th Somerset (Bath City) Battalion Home Guard in aid of the Funds of the Home Guard Organisation. (Authors)

Dances

Wartime dances were held anywhere there was room to foxtrot or do 'The Lambeth Walk': in church halls, factory canteens and local military bases. In Bath the main venues were the Pavilion, the Pump Room and the Assembly Rooms (until the latter was burnt out in the blitz of April 1942).

Sir Thomas Beecham's reservations about the architectural merits of the Pavilion were certainly not uppermost in people's minds on Tuesday and Friday evenings when the Pump Room Dance Orchestra (under the direction of Arthur Clark) was in residence at the Pavilion from 7.30 to 9.30. For 1s, or 6d for members of the armed forces wearing uniform, Bathonians could dance to the popular tunes of the period. On Saturday evenings from 7 until 9.45, Reg Ball and his Band took the stage at the Pavilion to allow Arthur Clark and his Orchestra to play at the weekly buffet dance held in the more architecturally desirable setting of the Pump Room. At this more formal event, uniform or evening dress was obligatory and a licensed buffet was available to dancers from 7.30 to 11.

Sport

When war broke out the Government banned all organised sport at which crowds might gather for fear of large casualties from bombing. But when the expected threat did not materialise, by October most major sports were reorganised on a wartime basis. At local level, many bowling clubs and cricket teams found their halls, greens and pitches requisitioned by the ARP or the Home Guard. For Bath's local rugby, soccer and cricket teams, many of their players had joined up and gone off to fight.

Soccer was reorganised nationally on the basis of eight local leagues. With the establishment of military camps in the vicinity of Bath, professional footballers who had joined up to serve in the forces and were stationed locally sought games with Bath City FC. As a result, there were some good opportunities during the war to watch a first-class game of football at Lambridge and later at Twerton Park. Under the capable stewardship of manager Arthur Mortimer, Bath City FC won the wartime League Cup and gates soared to more than 10,000 on many occasions. When Bath played Aston Villa at home in a qualifying game for the FA Cup, the gate was an incredible 17,000, but the teams drew 3–3. Sadly, one week later Bath lost 1–0 in the replay at Villa Park before a crowd of 30,000.

Among the Forces 'names' from national and international football who trod the hallowed turf at Bath were Vic Woodley and Johnny Jackson (both of whom played for Chelsea), Sid Low (Wales), Dave McCulloch (Scotland and Derby

Bath Rugby team: a wartime XV at their opening match of the season on the 'Rec' in 1942.

County), Bill Shankly (later to achieve fame as manager of Liverpool), and Stan Mortensen (England and Blackpool). A member of an RAF Sunderland flying boat crew, Mortensen was lucky when his aircraft was brought down in the Atlantic Ocean – he was rescued and survived to play another day.

Rugger suffered a shortage of players. In October 1941 it was reported in the *Chronicle* that because Bath RFC had failed to produce any matches that season, despite the fact that fixtures and many excellent players were available, Bath City FC should now play on the 'Rec'. However, in the same month, Bath RFC played a New Zealand XV and won by fourteen points to three. Three international 'caps' were in the Bath side in January 1942 when they met an RAF XV on the 'Rec': they were Gerrard (England), Shebean (Ireland) and D. Evans (Wales). In June the club received the good news that former Bath forward Major Peter Morley had been awarded the Military Cross.

Bath RFC benefited in the same way as its soccer counterpart from the presence of various military units in the neighbourhood, and the arrival of essential war workers from opposite sides of the country. There was no knowing who might turn up with their kit to play for a local side. The 1943 rugby season began with the *Chronicle* reporting plenty of players in the offing as well as a number of newcomers:

Lieutenant Mills, wing-three-quarter of Yorkshire, who played in the pack last season for Oxford Greyhounds; Hawkes, a forward from Birmingham University and Moseley; Lieutenant Norton RN, also a forward, and Lieutenant Lander centre-three-quarter from Notts, Lincs and Derby. John Wass, the Captain of Bath Rugby Club, will be away from Bath for the next three months on government business and in his absence Austin Higgins will take over.

The city's public baths attracted swimming clubs for sporting events, but for many Bathonians it was the simple pleasure of bathing that attracted them. These 'bathing belles' are enjoying a weekend dip at the Cleveland baths.

Tragedy hit the club in a number of ways throughout the war years. In February 1944 members learned that former Bath and Somerset forward Captain Peter Moon, who was also a Lansdown cricketer, had been killed in action in Italy fighting with the 8th Army, two days after his thirty-second birthday. In July came news that Lance-Corporal Leslie Philips, a former Bath rugby star-player, was reported missing in Normandy in the tough battle to break out from the beachhead after D-Day.

In that same year the future of postwar rugby in Bath was discussed. The two stands on the 'Rec' had been destroyed in the blitz of 1942 and the rebuilding of one of them was considered an indispensable preliminary to a return to a first-class fixture card. The possibility that Bath rugby should move to Lambridge was also considered for 'the transitional period from war to peace before one or both of the stands on the Recreation Ground' could be rebuilt, but the plan was turned down.

Soon after the end of the war in Europe in May 1945, sporting activities in Bath began gradually to return to normal. By the summer most of the players had returned and so too had the all-important supporters, all of whom looked forward to continuing with their respective sports after they had been so rudely interrupted by Hitler in 1939.

CHAPTER 11
Bath's Warrior Sons

When war broke out, hundreds of men from Bath were called up or volunteered to serve in Britain's armed forces at home and overseas. Others had joined up before the war and could boast many years of military service in peacetime. The ranks of the prewar 'regulars' in Britain's comparatively small but very professional Army, Navy and Air Force were soon swelled with the newcomers to the world of battledress and 'bull'.

Having said this, it might appear invidious on the part of the authors to single out just a handful of Bath's servicemen for special treatment, but to mention everyone who fought is simply impossible in a book of this size. Therefore, most of the men who follow have been chosen because their gallant exploits were recorded in the pages of the wartime *Chronicle*. What is noticeable in the wartime press is that a disproportionate amount of coverage was given to the Royal Air Force – equal to that given to the Army and Navy combined – and virtually nothing to the men of Britain's forgotten army in the Far East. The stories of the men who follow are a reflection of this fact.

BATH'S VICTORIA CROSS WINNER

Sergeant Tom Gray VC, RAF. On 11 June 1940, when the *London Gazette* announced the posthumous award of a Victoria Cross to Sergeant Thomas Gray,

an air observer, and his pilot flying officer, Donald Garland, the two men became the RAF's first VC winners of the Second World War. Gray's family lived at 2 Alexandra Place, Old Fosse Road, Odd Down, and the 25-year-old became Bath's one and only VC winner of the war.

Tom Gray had joined the RAF in 1929 and by the outbreak of war he was a sergeant air observer (navigator) flying in Fairey Battle light bombers with 12 Squadron. His squadron moved to France with the Advanced Air Striking Force but saw little activity throughout the first eight months of the 'Phoney War'. However, when Hitler launched his Blitzkrieg assaults against the Low Countries on 10 May 1940, 12 Squadron was flung into the breach.

On 12 May the squadron was chosen to undertake a 'suicide' mission to bomb bridges over the Albert Canal at Vroenhoven and Veldwezelt in Belgium in a last ditch effort to hold up the German advance. Five volunteer crews took off in the early morning, three to

Bath's posthumous VC, Sergeant Tom Gray. He was the first of three Gray brothers to die flying with the RAF during the Second World War. (Reg Gray)

bomb Veldwezelt and the others to attack Vroenhoven. Sergeant Tom Gray and Flying Officer Donald Garland, with a third crew member, LAC Lawrence Reynolds, as rear gunner, led the section of three Battles to attack the bridge at Veldwezelt.

Arriving in the target area, their Hurricane fighter escort had run into a 'crack' force of German Messerschmitt Bf 109 fighters. Fighting for their own survival, the Hurricanes were unable to provide protection for the Battles of 12 Squadron. Pressing home their attack from below 1,000 feet, Garland's section was met by a storm of flak hurled skywards from the hundreds of guns defending the vital bridge. Of the three aircraft in the section, one was set on fire and forced to jettison its bombs before making a force-landing nearby, another managed to drop its bombs on the target but was ripped to pieces by the murderous flak. Garland and Gray dived on the bridge and released their bombs but were shot down and crashed into the target area. All three crew were killed.

On 25 June 1941 the *Chronicle* reported that 'Bath parents receive son's VC. Hero of the canal bridge raid' at an investiture ceremony at Buckingham Palace. The words of the official citation revealed the bravery that led to the award of Britain's highest award for valour:

> Much of the success of this vital operation must be attributed to the formation leader, Flying Officer Garland, and to the coolness and resource of Sergeant Gray, who navigated Flying Officer Garland's aircraft under most difficult conditions in such a manner that the whole formation was able successfully to attack the target in spite of subsequent heavy losses.

But the price of patriotism was high for the Gray and Garland families: Tom Gray was the first of three brothers to die flying with the RAF during the Second World War, while Gerald Garland was the first of four to lose his life while in RAF service.

THE ROYAL AIR FORCE

The Battle of Britain that raged in the skies over southern England in the summer of 1940 witnessed the RAF's Spitfires and Hurricanes battling against the might of the Luftwaffe. Germany needed to seize control of the skies before launching an invasion on Britain, but the story of how the RAF's 'Few' fought the Luftwaffe's many and won against the odds has become an epic of modern history.

A handful of Bath men fought with distinction with the RAF during the battle, shooting down several enemy aircraft and achieving fame for their deeds. For every 'ace' there were dozens more pilots who flew and fought alongside them, but who did not receive the same glare of media publicity. This unsung majority bore the brunt of the action during the battle and without their resolve, and in many cases their sacrifice, victory could have gone to the Luftwaffe.

Pilot Officer Hilary Edridge. One of the unsung heroes of the Battle of Britain, as a 21-year-old Spitfire pilot with 222 Squadron Pilot Officer Hilary Edridge had fought over Dunkirk during the evacuation of the BEF in May and June 1940, shooting down a Bf 109 fighter plane. His squadron was in the thick of the action

THE BATTLE OF BRITAIN –
10 JULY TO 31 OCTOBER 1940

RAF Fighter Command: 1,020 aircraft destroyed, 537 pilots killed

Luftwaffe: 1,880 aircraft destroyed, 2,660 aircrew killed

during the Battle of Britain that followed: in August he was shot down over Kent by a Bf 109, baling out with burns to his face. On 20 October he shared in the destruction of a Bf 110, but on the 30th his Spitfire was severely damaged in combat with Bf 109s and crashed in flames when attempting to land. Edridge was rescued from the blazing wreckage but died of his injuries. His family lived at 29 Gay Street in the city.

As the war progressed, Bath produced its share of fighter aces – the 'ace' status being conferred on a pilot who has shot down at least five enemy aircraft.

One of 'The Few': Pilot Officer Hilary Edridge flew Spitfires in the Battle of Britain. He died from wounds received in action in October 1940. (Ione Denny)

Wing Commander Bob Braham DSO*, DFC*.
Credited with twenty-nine enemy aircraft destroyed and awarded three DSOs and three DFCs, Wing Commander Bob Braham from Holcombe near Bath was the RAF's highest scoring and most highly decorated nightfighter pilot of the war. The son of a Bath Methodist minister, Braham was a deadly practitioner of the art of nightfighting. He flew Bristol Beaufighters with 29 Squadron during the Luftwaffe's blitz on England, and later traded his 'Beau' for a de Havilland Mosquito with 141 Squadron in which he flew further afield on intruder sorties into France and on long-range patrols over the Bay of Biscay. He was shot down shortly after D-Day and spent the rest of the war as an unwilling guest of the Third Reich.

Squadron Leader James Maclachlan DSO, DFC*. In May 1943 one-armed Old Monktonian fighter ace Squadron Leader James Maclachlan opened the school's 'Wings for Victory Week'. Two months later he crash-landed his burning North American Mustang fighter in a field near Dieppe but died from his injuries days later in a German hospital.

Maclachlan saw his first action as an RAF bomber pilot in France during the desperate spring of 1940 but transferred to Fighter Command in June and fought throughout the Battle of Britain. He was posted overseas to the besieged island of Malta in the autumn where, flying a Hurricane with 261 Squadron, he bagged eight enemy aircraft in a month. In February 1941 the tables were turned on him when he was shot down by a German fighter, baling out with his left arm shattered by a cannon shell. Although doctors battled in vain to save his left

One-armed fighter ace Squadron Leader James Maclachlan shot down more than sixteen enemy aircraft before he was killed in action in July 1943. (Authors)

forearm they were forced to amputate but, undeterred by his injury, Maclachlan was back flying again within three weeks. He returned to England, where he was fitted with an artificial limb, and, by now in command of 1 Squadron, he continued to add to his score of enemy aircraft. Joining the Air Fighting Development Unit in June 1943, he and a fellow Mustang pilot shot down six enemy aircraft in ten minutes during a fight that took place south of Paris. However, on a similar sortie on 18 July James Maclachlan met his end, aged just twenty-four. Maclachlan held the DSO and DFC and Bar, and his final tally of enemy aircraft stood at 16, with 1 shared, 1 possible and 3 damaged.

Wing Commander Johnny Baldwin DSO*, DFC*. The dynamic wartime career of Wing Commander Johnny Baldwin, whose family were bombed out of their home at Green Park in the Bath blitz, had a humble beginning. Enlisting as an airman in 1939, Baldwin served as groundcrew and on bomb disposal duties during the London blitz before volunteering for pilot training. He joined his first squadron, No. 609, in November 1942 and shot down his first enemy aircraft after just four hours flying Hawker Typhoons. Details of his antics over Paris on 2 January 1944 appeared next day in the *Chronicle* and made good copy:

Bath Pilot chased Nazis Around Eiffel Tower

Afternoon strollers in Paris on Sunday saw the extraordinary spectacle of four RAF Typhoons led by a Bath pilot chasing a number of German aircraft around the Eiffel Tower, shooting as they went. The chase was led by Squadron Leader John Robert Baldwin, 26-year-old only son of Mr and Mrs C. Baldwin, of 30 Grosvenor, Bath.

'We were looking for trouble,' he said, 'there was heavy cloud right down on the deck until we were 30 miles inside France. Then the cloud cleared and presently we saw 12 Messerschmitts on an airfield. They were wearing desert camouflage and we shot them up. We left a number of them smoking after each of the Typhoons had made two attacks.'

The Typhoons went on towards Paris and suddenly came across a German training school. The Buecker 131 training aircraft were doing acrobatics when the Typhoons appeared amongst them. A chase developed in which the training biplanes flew round and round the Eiffel Tower and the Typhoons flew after them. One of the Buecker 131's was destroyed by a Canadian pilot.

On the way home the Typhoons encountered a FW 190 which Squadron Leader Baldwin shot down with an unusually short burst of some 20 rounds of cannon fire.

Typhoon pilot Squadron Leader Johnny Baldwin was one of the RAF's most flamboyant fighter aces of the war, claiming fifteen enemy aircraft destroyed. He was posted missing in action during the Korean War in 1952. (Paul Lashmar)

It is believed Baldwin led the group of eight Typhoons that attacked a vehicle convoy in France on 17 July 1944, wounding Field Marshal Erwin Rommel – the legendary 'Desert Fox'. He went on to win two DSOs and two DFCs, and shot down fifteen enemy aircraft, but was posted missing in action during the Korean War in 1952 while on attachment to the USAF flying F-86 Sabre jet fighters. To this day his fate remains unknown.

Squadron Leader Lewis Brandon DSO, DFC*. 'Double DFC for Donat's Double' was how the *London Evening Standard* reported RAF nightfighter radar operator Lewis Brandon's latest bravery award in 1944. Brandon, from Bath, bore such a striking resemblance to film star Robert Donat that he was chosen by film directors to be his screen stand-in and appeared in many of his movies, of which *Goodbye Mr Chips* was undoubtedly the most famous.

Off the screen, Squadron Leader Lewis Brandon and his pilot, Wing Commander James Benson, became a successful RAF nightfighter crew. Between them they bagged 10 enemy aircraft, damaged 4 more, and destroyed 6 V1 Flying Bombs. Brandon and Benson teamed up on 141 Squadron in mid-1941 to fly

Beaufighter nightfighters on home defence duties. They later swapped the 'Beau' for the Mosquito which they flew to great effect with 157 Squadron on roving nightfighter patrols and intruder sorties into occupied Europe and patrols over the Bay of Biscay. Awarded the DSO in 1945, after the war Brandon wrote about his wartime experiences in *Night Flyer*.

Pilot Officer J.H. Toone DFC, DFM. The demise of one of the most promising RAF nightfighter crews of the war was recorded in the *Chronicle* on 19 November 1942.

Pilot Officer Toone (of Bath) Killed – 'Salt and Pepper', Ace Night Fighters, Crash

Members of one of the best nightfighter teams of the RAF, Flying Officer George Pepper DFC, and Pilot Officer J.H. Toone DFM, of Bath, have been killed in a flying accident in Britain.

'Salt and Pepper', as they were known, flew together for six months, taking part in many operations in which they displayed initiative and perfect teamwork. This month they shot down three enemy raiders in one night. Flying Officer Pepper, a Canadian, was the former West Ham dirt track star and TT motorcyclist. Pilot Officer Toone was, before the war, a director of Sydney W. Bush & Son Ltd, the well known Bath provisions store. He thus became 'salt' to his companion's 'pepper'.

'Pepper and Salt': Flying Officer George Pepper and Pilot Officer Harry Toone, of Bath (right), with a piece of a Dornier Do 217 (4255, U5+PK, of 2/KG2) which they shot down in their Beaufighter on 31 October/1 November 1942. (Catherine Alley)

They had six night raiders to their credit and one probable, while their performance on that Saturday night was the second occasion only on which the 'hat trick' had been performed over Britain.

For their 'hat trick' during the night of 31 October/1 November 1942, when the 29 Squadron Beaufighter crew claimed three Dornier Do 217 bombers shot down in two sorties, Pepper was awarded a Bar to his DFC and Toone (of 13 Hensley Road) a DFC, but by the time the awards were officially announced in the press on 11 December, 'Salt and Pepper' were dead, killed in a flying accident during a daylight test flight near Detling in Kent on 17 November. Had they lived it is certain they would have added considerably to their score.

Flight Lieutenant R.F.W. Turner DFC. The crew of the RAF Lancaster bomber in which Flight Lieutenant R.F.W. Turner DFC of 27 Royal Crescent was rear gunner boasted a shared total of 330 operational sorties and five bravery awards. But even this impressive wealth of experience failed to prevent the Pathfinder crew from 83 Squadron falling victim to the deadly defences in the night skies over Berlin.

On the night of 23/24 August 1943, Turner's Lancaster bomber, callsign 'A for Apple', was caught in searchlights over the German capital during a devastating attack by more than 700 RAF heavy bombers. 'A for Apple' was quickly spotted by a prowling German nightfighter and shot down in flames. From the crew of seven, only Turner survived to become a prisoner-of-war in the notorious Stalag Luft 3 camp at Sagan in Silesia. He was one of seventy-six men who attempted the 'Great Escape' in March 1944. Although Turner himself was unsuccessful in his bid for freedom, he was fortunate that he lived to tell the tale unlike fifty of his fellow escapees who were murdered in cold blood by the Gestapo. The camp was liberated by American troops on 29 April 1945 and Turner finally returned home to Bath on 26 May.

THE ARMY

Lance Corporal William Manns. On 13 February 1940 the *Chronicle* recorded Bath's first military casualty of the war. Lance Corporal William Manns, of the 8th Battalion, Worcestershire Regiment and whose home was at 55 First Avenue, Oldfield Park, had died on active service after only three weeks in France. He was twenty-one. Before joining up in July 1939 he had been a clerk in the Town Clerk's office at the Guildhall. The *Chronicle* reported:

> The War Office were unable to accede to the request of the parents that the body of L/Cpl Manns should be conveyed home for burial. At the funeral service overseas, four of his personal friends acted as bearers and his most intimate friends walked immediately behind the coffin to represent the relatives.

Lance Corporal James Fairchild MM, RASC. While the tired and tattered remnants of the British Expeditionary Force were being evacuated from Dunkirk's beaches in May 1940 by flotillas of ships great and small, many individual acts of selflessness and bravery were played out against the scream of Stuka dive-bombers and the thud of exploding bombs. One of the heroes of Dunkirk was Lance Corporal James Fairchild RASC, from 17 Croft Road,

Fairfield Park, whose heroism in attacking three German aircraft in the evacuation from Dunkirk was rewarded with the Military Medal. Nine months later a report in the *Chronicle* of 15 February 1941 revealed the incredible story:

How Bath Man Won M.M.: Heroically Attacked Three Nazi Planes

Lance Corporal Fairchild, who is a former employee of the Bath Tramway Co. Ltd, was in charge of a Bren gun on a lorry in the Dunkirk evacuation. Suddenly three German dive-bombers appeared and proceeded to drop their deadly cargo in the vicinity of the lorry. Remaining at his post alone, Fairchild opened fire on the three planes who directed their attention on him.

After his first burst of fire the three planes disappeared and later two returned, one securing a direct hit on the lorry, just after Fairchild had got off.

His adventures were only just beginning, however, for Lance Corporal Fairchild had again to face intense bombing on his return to this country in a steamer. The ship became waterlogged and Fairchild found himself in the sea. He was only able to save his life by swimming to a submarine in which he was conveyed to this country.

However, the hand of fate dealt cruel blows against two other Bath soldiers who had been plucked from under the noses of the triumphant German Army at Dunkirk. Lance Corporal Claude Gray RAOC, of Lynwood, Fairfield Road, was killed by enemy action in the Channel off Dover, minutes away from setting foot again on English soil; while on 8 June Military Policeman Lance Corporal Harry Sweet, of Odd Down, was on his way home to Bath to see his wife when he was crushed between a motor vehicle and a wall at Frome and fatally injured – days after being rescued from Dunkirk.

Lance Corporal Claude Gray was killed by enemy action when being evacuated from Dunkirk in May 1940.

Corporal Philip Comm DCM. As the Allied armies fought their way into Germany in the spring of 1945, a Bath soldier with the 43rd Wessex Division was caught up in a desperate battle at an insignificant north German village called Vehlingen. He was Corporal Philip Comm, a platoon commander with 7th Battalion, the Somerset Light Infantry. After the huge airborne and amphibious crossing of the Rhine by Allied troops on 26 March, the SLI was part of a force ordered to secure a partially constructed Autobahn at Vehlingen between the villages of Millingen and Anholt on the 27th. The Autobahn was heavily defended by crack *Panzergrenadier* and *Fallschirmjäger* (parachute) troops and its possession was finally secured at a heavy cost in British and German lives. It was not until one month after the war had ended that Comm's bravery under fire and his award of the DCM was reported in the *Chronicle*:

OPERATION 'DYNAMO' – 26 MAY TO 4 JUNE 1940

The evacuation of Allied troops by sea from Dunkirk:
Total rescued: 364,628 – 224,686 British, 139,942 French and Belgian
Allied shipping losses: 200 vessels of all types
Allied aircraft losses: 177

Turned Whole Line: Gallant Bath Corporal Wins DCM

A fortnight or so ago we announced that the Distinguished Conduct Medal had been awarded to Corporal Philip Anthony Comm, the Somerset Light Infantry, of Bath, for service in North West Europe. The citation now published shows that this distinction has come to him for courage and resource which had the effect of turning an entire enemy defence line. The citation states:

'On 27th March 1945 Cpl Comm commanded the leading section of a forward platoon in an attack on the Autobahn at Vehlingen. The advance was stopped short of the objective by heavy machine gun fire from several well-dug-in and mutually supported posts and Cpl Comm's section suffered casualties.

'He at once brought accurate fire to bear on the enemy; himself got the wounded back, continued to neutralise the opposition, and indicated the positions to the supporting tanks. Under the tanks' fire this NCO then led his section forward under a hail of criss-crossing enemy bullets. He then, by bold and clever use of ground, crawled right up to the enemy defences and got to close quarters. Thirty Boche gave themselves up; several were dead.

'Through brave and skilful advance under exceptionally heavy fire at once enabled flanking platoons to advance and close with the enemy. Cpl Comm's gallantry, initiative and leadership without a doubt turned the whole enemy defence line consisting of an ideal position and trenches full of ammunition.'

CASUALTIES SUFFERED BY 4TH AND 7TH BATTALIONS, THE SOMERSET LIGHT INFANTRY

NW Europe campaign – 24 June 1944 to 5 May 1945: 468 killed in action (inc 30 officers), 2,493 injured

Corporal Philip Comm, Somerset Light Infantry, was awarded an immediate DCM for bravery in helping to capture enemy positions in Germany in March 1945. He is seen here at the investiture of his award by Field Marshal Montgomery. (Philip Comm)

THE ROYAL NAVY

On 17 September the elderly 22,500-ton aircraft carrier HMS *Courageous* became the first Allied warship to be lost to enemy action in the Second World War. *Courageous* was torpedoed and sunk by the German U-boat *U-29* in the Atlantic Ocean off south-west Ireland with the loss of 519 of her 1,260-strong crew, of which five were from Bath:

Casualties in *Courageous*: Local Men Reported Lost

We learn that among those reported to have been lost in HMS *Courageous* were Percy Walter Minns (44) of 48 Ivy Avenue. A pensioner in the RNR he was a Bath postman highly respected by staff and public. John Edward Keeling (39) of 3 Odd Down Terrace, a widower who was due to have left the Navy in August. Victor Lawley (26) of 35 Green Park, was only lately transferred to the *Courageous*. He has one sister and three brothers and was a nephew of Mr Ernest Freeman, the well-known Bath cricketer. Edward Bath (31) of 1 Oxford Terrace, Combe Down, married with two young children, he was formerly a garage and taxi proprietor. Ronald Pritchard (23) of 11 Clement Street had joined the Navy as a boy.

Royal Marine Reginald Turner. On 14 October 1939, with the war barely a month old, another elderly British battleship, the 29,500-ton HMS *Royal Oak*, was sunk in a daring attack by the German U-boat *U-47* in the British Home Fleet anchorage at Scapa Flow in the Orkneys. An admiral and 832 of *Royal Oak*'s crew went to the bottom with her. The loss of this veteran warship made little difference to the Allies' superiority at sea, but the effect on morale at home was enormous. One of the few lucky survivors was a Bath man, 33-year-old father of three Royal Marine Reginald Turner of 31 Thomas Street, Walcot. The *Chronicle* carried a graphic interview with Turner in its edition of 24 October:

SIX REPORTED TO HAVE GONE DOWN

Tom Curtis | Victor Lawley | Ronald Pritchard
John Edward Keeling | Robert Bath | Percy Walter Minns

Six local men, including five from Bath, were reported lost when the aircraft carrier HMS Courageous *was torpedoed and sunk by a German U-boat in the Atlantic in September 1939.*

I was asleep in my hammock and was awakened by a dull explosion about 1.5am on Oct. 14th. The next and heavier explosion came about 1.15 and then the ship began to tilt over badly. There was no panic at all, but we had to be quick and jump over the side of the vessel which was heeling over badly by then.

Some accounts of the sinking said that it was fairly light, but actually it was pitch dark at the time with not much of a tide.

With men all around me in the water, I managed to hold on to the side and then swim away; five minutes later the *Royal Oak* was sunk in a terrific flurry of water.

I swam about for a little while and then heard men singing. I didn't believe the stories of men singing while waiting to be picked up, but there was a vessel nearby called *Daisy* and the men were singing 'Daisy, Daisy'. It was extraordinary.

Soon afterwards the survivors were picked up, Reginald Turner with them, and taken on board a neighbouring vessel. Once ashore, the men were taken to Thurso.

Leading Seaman Reginald Legg DSM. As already mentioned, the epic evacuation from Dunkirk saw many courageous acts from selfless individuals, servicemen and civilians alike. One such hero was Leading Seaman Reginald Legg of Kingsmead East, who was a crewman on HM Skoot *Twente* (a skoot is a shallow draught coastal craft, not unlike a Thames barge in appearance). From late on 28 May to the early evening of the 31st, the *Twente* and its crew shuttled back and forth across the Channel between the Kent port of Ramsgate and the blazing ruins of Dunkirk, enduring frequent air attack, to rescue a total of more than 1,500 troops from the harbour.

On the afternoon of the 29th the paddle steamer HMS *Gracie Fields* had just embarked 750 troops from the beach at La Panne when she was bombed and seriously damaged. Scalding steam escaping from broken pipes engulfed her crowded upper deck, adding to the death and carnage following a bomb strike amidships. With her rudder jammed the stricken steamer became a sitting target for Stuka dive-bombers as she circled helplessly and endlessly. With complete disregard for their own safety the masters of HM Skoots *Twente* and *Jutland*, while still underway, tied up tight alongside the vessel so their crews could take off survivors before she finally sank.

For his gallantry during this daring rescue, Leading Seaman Legg was awarded the DSM. This is what the Navy's official citation said:

Royal Marine Reginald Turner was one of the survivors from HMS Royal Oak *that was sunk by a U-boat at Scapa Flow, less than a month after the loss of* Courageous.

Hero of the Dunkirk evacuation: Leading Seaman Reginald Legg was responsible, with others, for the rescue of more than 1,500 Allied troops from the French harbour. For his 'coolness and resource under fire' Legg was awarded the DSM.

Leading Seaman Reginald Legg displayed coolness and resource under fire during the several trips as coxswain of the *Twente* and later in the motor launch *Kestrel*. He was largely responsible for the successful rescues from the sinking *Gracie Fields* by his seamanlike actions. His conduct at all times was admirable.

In January 1943 the *Chronicle* reported Legg 'missing believed killed in a recent action'. By then he had been promoted to the rank of petty officer and was serving with the destroyer HMS *Firedrake* engaged on North Atlantic convoy protection duties between Britain and the USA. During the night of 17 December 1942 *Firedrake* was torpedoed and sunk in mountainous seas by *U-211*, 600 miles south of Iceland, with heavy loss of life – including that of Reginald Legg.

Captain Frederick Parham DSO, RN. Later Admiral Sir Frederick, Captain Frederick Parham RN, of 18 Sion Hill, commanded the heavy cruiser HMS *Belfast* during the dramatic chase and destruction of the German battlecruiser *Scharnhorst* by ships of the Home Fleet in the icy seas off the North Cape of Norway on Boxing Day 1943. The *Scharnhorst*'s denouement was acted out in atrocious weather conditions of bitter cold, rough seas and pale daylight inside the Arctic circle. The *Chronicle* of 5 January 1944 carried a lengthy report of the action and an interview with Captain Parham:

Bath Captain's Dramatic Story of 'Kill' –
Tense Moments When Enemy Seemed Likely to 'Stand and Fight'
'For a moment it looked as if the *Scharnhorst* was going to stand and fight. Then he appeared to lose his nerve, and turned tail and fled.' Later Captain Parham said he was certain his ship had one torpedo hit on the *Scharnhorst*. Captain Parham said: 'As far as the cruisers were concerned, the action was divided into three phases. The first was brief. we made contact with a large unidentified vessel which was obviously the *Scharnhorst*, and *Norfolk* opened fire, while we fired star shells. The enemy did not return the fire and eventually sheered off.

'The Admiral now made his big decision – to get back to the convoy so as to be certain of being there to protect it after *Scharnhorst* had worked away to the northward if she came in again. This was exactly what she did.

'Later, when we were in position on the convoy's bow, contact was made again. All three cruisers opened fire, and the Admiral, in accordance with his previously thought out plan, turned the squadron in line abreast head-on to the enemy and we rode at him at full speed.

'For a moment it looked as if the *Scharnhorst* was going to stand and fight. Then he appeared to lose his nerve, and turned tail and fled. The cruisers followed after him, and both sides were firing away with their main armament. Red points of light showed that we were scoring hits. It was about this time that the *Norfolk* was hit. No shots fell near us and only the flashes of her guns told us that the *Scharnhorst* was firing. What we had prayed for was happening. The *Scharnhorst* was sailing away from the convoy – and (what she did not know) running straight into the arms of the *Duke of York*.'

When the end finally came it was night and the German battlecruiser was pounded by gunfire from *Belfast* and the battleship *Duke of York*, and by torpedoes

Lance Sergeant Bert Smith and Gunner Frank Brown, both of the Maritime Artillery, sailed on the doomed Arctic Convoy PQ17 in June 1942. Their ships were sunk by enemy action and they escaped with their lives, adrift for eight days in an open boat in the Arctic Ocean. (Frank Brown/Bath Chronicle)

from supporting destroyers. At 1945 hr *Scharnhorst* exploded and slid beneath the icy black waters, with only thirty-six survivors from her crew of more than 2,000 men. For his part in the action, Parham was awarded an immediate DSO.

Lance Sergeant Bert Smith DSM and Gunner Frank Brown RA. To the men who sailed with the Merchant Marine and Royal Navy on the notorious Arctic supply convoys to the north Russian ports of Arkhangelsk and Murmansk, the experiences of Captain Parham at North Cape would have been familiar. But for them, added to the threats of freezing weather conditions, mountainous seas and U-boat attack was the extra fear of attack from German surface raiders and land-based dive-bombers.

In January 1943 the *Chronicle* reported that a Bath man, Lance Sergeant Bert Smith, who was an Army gunner on a merchant ship in convoy bound for Russia, had been awarded the DSM for devotion to duty. Although no explanation was given in this edition of the paper or in the *London Gazette* (in which official notices of awards to servicemen were published), a report that had appeared on 7 September the previous year gave the chilling background to the story:

Eight Days in an Open Boat – Ordeal for Two Bath Men
Recovering at his home, 3 Shaftesbury Avenue, Lower Weston, from the effects of eight days in an open boat in the Arctic on a diet of biscuits and water is 20-years-old Gunner Frank Brown RA (Maritime AA). With another man, Sergeant Bert Smith, also of the Maritime AA, whose home is at 9 Grove Street, Frank

Black smoke billowing skywards marks the end of an Allied merchantman sailing with an Arctic supply convoy. (Authors)

went through the continuous four days bombing attack on an Allied convoy to one of Russia's Arctic ports. With him in the boat after their ship had gone down were 36 other men. They remained in it for eight days with nothing but biscuits and water to fortify them against the terrible Arctic cold.

Fifty miles from the Russian coast a Soviet trawler picked them up. Frank was taken straight to a Russian hospital suffering from exposure. He spent some four weeks in that country. Sergeant Smith whose ship was also sunk was rescued earlier than Frank.

The two men had sailed from Iceland with Convoy PQ17 in June 1942, bound for the north Russian port of Arkhangelsk. Frank Brown had embarked on the 5,203-ton freighter *Bolton Castle*, which was carrying a deadly cargo of cordite in her main hold. In one of the greatest tragedies of the Second World War, PQ17 had been ordered to scatter by Admiral Dudley Pound because it seemed to the First Sea Lord that, contrary to intelligence advice, heavy German surface forces were sailing against it.

In fact, the big ships had never sailed and the thirty-four merchantmen of PQ17, by now alone and undefended after their escort destroyers had fled, were scattered across the unforgiving Barents Sea more than 400 miles inside the Arctic Circle. They were picked off in turn by German dive-bombers and U-boats, which between them sent a total of twenty-three ships to the bottom of the freezing ocean. This included the *Bolton Castle*, attacked by eight Junkers Ju 88 dive-bombers. One bomb penetrated her No. 2 hold, which contained the volatile cargo of cordite, and the ensuing explosion tore a gaping hole in her hull. *Bolton Castle*'s blazing hulk slowly stood up on end and sank, but mercifully all of her crew, including Frank Brown, got away safely in the two lifeboats.

CHAPTER 12
'The Road to Victory'

Christmas 1944 was one of the coldest periods on record. In Bath there was no snow, but the *Chronicle* recorded that a 'lacework of ice had spread over trees and covered telegraph and aerial wires with needles of dazzling frost, and produced as white a Christmas as had there been a snowstorm'. Across the Channel in eastern Belgium the Battle of the Bulge was in full spate with the Germans making a last desperate bid to drive a wedge through the Allied advance, recapture Paris and cut off their main supply port of Antwerp. Only a tough round of fighting by the Allied armies in the harsh winter snows of the Ardennes forest managed to turn the tide and push the Germans back, before the Allied advance into Germany could be resumed.

As sixth new year of the war, 1945 was 'seen in' across the city with the usual traditional dances but this time with the fervent hope that it would be the last new year celebrated under war conditions. Adding an extra contribution to festivities the Parkside British Restaurant opened its doors every weekday until 9 p.m., and on three Saturdays in January, February and March it held dances from 7 to 10 p.m. with music provided by Lew Davies and her Boys. Admission to the 'dance enclosure' was 6*d*. Across the city at the Pavilion, dancers could enjoy the music of the Royal Air Force Bomber Command Dance Orchestra, under the direction of 'Britain's radio ace' Sergeant Leslie Douglas. 'Help the Wounded and Enjoy Yourself at the Dance' exhorted a newspaper advertisement for George Woodfield's Gay Nineties and Modern Dance Orchestra, also appearing at the Pavilion.

With another severe frost, 23 January was said to have been Bath's coldest night for years, although the sub-zero temperatures failed to deter young skaters who were to be seen on the canal, which had been frozen solid for some time. Temperatures continued to drop and four days later it was reported that Bath was in the grip of the second coldest spell since 1899, with bitter weather and heavy snow. The bitterly cold weather had lasted with hardly a break since Christmas Eve, and some elderly residents said that they had known nothing like it since the famous winter of 1892.

As the chill of winter began to recede, thoughts on the postwar evolution of the city began to occupy the minds of the city's planners. Sir Patrick Abercrombie's 'Plan for Bath' was unveiled to the public at the beginning of February in an exhibition of models, maps, drawings and photographs. The far-sighted plan was concerned with not only the building of new houses and conversion of older ones in the city, but also the routing of traffic and proposals for public and industrial buildings.

On 14 February came news of the terrible 'double night blitz' on the east German city of Dresden. Eight hundred RAF heavy bombers unloaded more than 2,600 tons of incendiaries and high explosives onto the city; at least 50,000 inhabitants were killed in the firestorm that ensued. Two days later the *Chronicle* reported that 'something tremendous' was unfolding as a prelude to the invasion of Japan – 1,500 American bombers attacked Tokyo with 'the greatest fleet ever flaunting the enemy in their front yard'. The tide had truly turned in favour of

Part of a model used to illustrate Patrick Abercrombie's Plan for Bath, *1945. Only a few of his proposals materialised as they had been originally envisaged. C – Cultural Centre, D – Shopping and business premises; F – Lido; G – Riverside Café; J – Business premises.*

the Allies, who were now unleashing massive destruction on Germany and Japan on a scale previously unimagined.

Easter Day 1945 fell on All Fools' Day (1 April) and large numbers of Bath residents descended upon the city's two railway stations, having decided to go away for what was likely to be the last Easter of the war in Europe. On 4 April it was reported that elements of Monty's 21st Army Group were less than 45 miles from the north German city of Hanover, but most of Holland had been virtually cut off by the Germans and much of her civilian population was in danger of starving to death. The roads were crammed with Dutch refugees, pouring east from the German-occupied pocket in western Holland. Meanwhile, the *Chronicle* reported 'end of world' scenes in burning north-west German cities, the mystery fires believed to be the result of a scorched earth policy by the Nazis who were determined that the Allies would possess only a ruined land.

Towards the end of April the lights went on again all over Britain for the first time since the outbreak of war. No longer were residents obliged to draw their blinds and curtains for the black-out. In Bath, the heights at Beechen Cliff proved to be a fine vantage point from which to view this momentous occasion.

As Bath began to 'wind down', static water tanks provided for fire fighting purposes were removed from streets, squares and parks around the city. But the war was still being fought, as the public continued to be reminded by Savings advertisements: 'We're thanking those fighting lads of ours by keeping our weekly War Savings right up to scratch. Let's save as hard as they fight!'

Hitler committed suicide on 30 April as his 'Thousand-Year Reich' crumbled and burned around him – it had lasted just twelve years. Berlin fell to

overwhelming Russian forces soon after, and victory in Europe came at last on 7 May 1945 when Admiral Doenitz, Hitler's successor, offered unconditional surrender of all German forces on all fronts to General Eisenhower, effective from 0001 hr on 9 May. Europe was suddenly at peace, but the war in the Far East against Japan was stepped up. The citizens of Bath took to the streets overnight and there were bonfires and rejoicings to celebrate VE-Day:

People in Bath started celebrating VE-Day on Monday evening – many in fact commenced in the afternoon when the news became known. Faces lit up when copies of the *Bath and Wilts Chronicle* appeared on the streets and papers sold like wildfire. 'It isn't that we have forgotten the war in the Far East' said one citizen, 'but there is the joyful realisation that never again, we hope, shall we hear the sirens'. Even though the situation has been easier lately, there has always been the possibility in the minds of many people that their night's rest might be disturbed by the 'banshee'. Now at last it is all over in Bath, London and everywhere in the country. Apart from that there is the thought that the slaughter in Europe is finished and that before very long we shall be welcoming our boys back, in many cases for good.

Flags appeared on the city streets on Monday afternoon. One Bath householder who bought a number of flags of all nations at an auction sale just before the war has announced his intention was to keep them until VE-Day. Many people hung out flags and emblems that they saved from the coronation.

Newsboys on Monday afternoon were shouting 'Victory Paper' instead of their usual 'War News, Latest!'. Bonfires were lighted in some parts of the city on Monday night. There were some in the Englishcombe and Southdown

Customers eager to purchase the Victory in Europe edition of the Chronicle *from Mr Biggs at the corner of Westgate Street on 7 May 1945.*

districts, and there was even one at Grosvenor Place on the strip of green in front of the houses. Said a Bath housewife to her spouse this morning: 'I haven't heard the German signature tune broadcast yet'. Said her husband, 'What's that?' Said his better half, 'I surrender, dear!'.

Many civil servants got trains to London on Monday night, others followed by the first available trains this morning.

Upper Weston festivities did not end until one o'clock this morning. The whole village has been decorated with a large 'V' sign being erected. This contains a picture of Mr Churchill surmounted by the words 'Weston Thanks You'.

The *Chronicle*'s leading article talked of a 'golden day of victory':

Today, VE-Day, the world is enjoying itself for, as we were able to write in this column of our later editions yesterday, the war against Germany has been won. Everywhere the flags and the bunting are flying, from the mansion requisitioned for the purposes of total war down to the humblest cottage – and the bomb-scarred site which was once a happy home and would be still but for the evil which Germany wrought . . .

Spontaneous celebrations in and around the city led to a run on cigarettes and beer at tobacconists and in public houses:

Cigarette Shortage

Public houses in the city and district were crowded on Monday night. For most of them it was 'beer only'. Fresh supplies arrived at many houses this morning. A number of tobacconists had run out of cigarettes by the middle of the morning, so heavy was the run on their stock.

The Prime Minister's broadcast was relayed during a break in the programme at the Beau Nash cinema this afternoon, and the King's speech will similarly be heard by the audience at 9 pm. Police permission has been obtained for an extension loudspeaker to be fixed outside the cinema so that speeches may be heard by people in the street.

'One man celebrated too soon,' said Detective Inspector T. Coles at Bath Magistrates Court when John McIlmurray of Hawthorn was charged with being drunk and incapable in Southgate Street at 3 o'clock on Monday afternoon.

There were unforgettable scenes as Bath celebrated VE-Night with bonfires, processions and singing in the streets. The *Chronicle* of 9 May reported:

With bonfires blazing in streets where uglier fires had crackled and glowed three years ago, with song and joyfulness and with hearts uplifted in solemn thanksgiving, Bath celebrated VE-Day. From morn til night great crowds were everywhere watching impromptu fancy-dress processions, taking part in impromptu singing, watching effigies of Hitler consumed by flames in a score and more parts of the city. Streets were packed. Self-consciousness and reserve vanished on VE-Night. People of all classes mingled in common rejoicing. The officialdom of our always helpful policemen was at a minimum.

Twerton residents in fancy dress celebrate Victory in Europe.

The war in Europe was over, the war in the Far East, everyone fervently hoped, would soon be over too. One of the most moving and typical scenes illustrating that while everybody was happy no one abused the occasion to make a nuisance of himself, was the scene at the bottom of Milsom Street at midnight where hundreds of people sang in the roadway watching the six flaming torches on the Bath Gas Company's building. As midnight struck, the torches flickered and went out leaving only the traffic lights for illumination. A sudden hush descended on the concourse, then someone started singing 'Land of Hope and Glory'. It was taken up by everyone and standing there in the roadway and on the pavements they sang Arthur Benson's verses which expressed so well their hopes and faith in the future.

It wasn't far off midnight. When we arrived at the Old Bridge the electricity showrooms were floodlit and hundreds of people were dancing in the roadway. 'The Lambeth Walk' was the most popular with 'The Palais Glide' running it a close second. It was midnight when the showrooms in Old Bond Street closed and a great shout of disappointment went up from the tightly packed crowd as the six gas-burning flares went out at twelve. To that

Residents of Hampton Row with celebratory cakes before starting their street party.

point the crowd was singing and dancing, and one man with a ukulele was a great favourite. It was an unforgettable picture.

It was surprising how many people in the Abbey Church Yard were just content to stare at the floodlit west door of the Abbey, a sight of which they had been deprived for five years and eight months. We took one last look, and one last picture of this most memorable night, and then went home. It had been a good day – one which we all deserved.

A service of thanksgiving was held at the Abbey and a Victory Parade to mark the end of six long years of war. The Civil Defence stand-down parade was held on Sunday 10 June, followed by a service at the Abbey.

Looking to the future, Bath's 60,000 voters now turned their attention to the forthcoming General Election. Churchill's wartime coalition government had done its job and the time had come to return to the cut and thrust of normal political life. Bath's new voting register was up by several thousand on its prewar total: civilian resident voters numbered 54,827, while Admiralty officials employed overseas from Bath, merchant seamen and others accounted for a further 4,698 voters.

On 26 July, following the General Election, it was announced that an 'anti-Churchill vote' had won, resulting in a House of Commons majority against the Government. At Bath a vigorous campaign had been waged with the result that I.J. Pitman (Conservative) was elected with a slim majority of 2,076. (In the previous General Election in 1935, the Conservative majority was 12,020.)

Cllr Edgar Clements (Mayor of Bath) takes the salute outside the Guildhall at the stand-down parade of the Civil Defence in June 1945.

Mrs D. Archibald (Labour) came a close second with 18,120, and Major Philip Hopkins (Liberal) polled 7,952 votes.

Meanwhile, the war in the Far East against Japan continued unabated. In July the Japs were bombed around the clock with 1,000 American bomber aircraft attacking almost simultaneously in a concentrated strike. There were plans to continue bombing them day and night in an effort to break their stubborn resistance.

When the first atom bomb ever to be used in warfare was dropped on Hiroshima on 6 August, it seared all living things to death with an awesome power and destructiveness previously unimagined. The devastated Japanese city was reduced to a wasteland and the 80,000 dead scorched beyond recognition. Despite the dropping of a second atom bomb on Nagasaki three days later, the Japanese still refused to surrender and only after a threat by the Allies to 'unleash fury' did the Emperor finally agree to a ceasefire. The Crown Prince, who was said to have threatened death to Allied airmen, was appointed to head a new Tokyo cabinet.

On 14 August Emperor Hirohito announced that his government would accept the terms demanded by the Allies for ending the war. At midnight, when Churchill broadcast to the nation that Japanese forces had surrendered unconditionally, Bath erupted into a spontaneous outburst of celebration. Next day's *Chronicle* reported the incredible scenes witnessed on the city streets during the night:

Convalescent soldiers at St Martin's Hospital pose for the camera on VJ-Day. (Bob White)

Bath Overjoyed by V-J News
Midnight Peace Thrill

Huge crowds thronged Bath streets from shortly after midnight when the V-J news 'broke', until the early hours of this morning, singing, dancing and celebrating.

Having heard the momentous announcement by the Premier on the midnight news, people swarmed out of doors. Neighbours were hastily roused from sleep and scores of folk did not stop to dress – they just flung dressing gowns over their night attire and joined the throng. A few minutes after midnight two Admiralty cars went screaming through the city, their motor horns waking more and more people.

American soldiers had earlier come into Bath to spend the evening. They were about to return to camp in two large lorries when the news came. People climbed on to the lorries which made a tour of the city.

British servicemen joined arms and danced in the streets. Some of them clanged salvage bin lids by way of accompaniment. Huge crowds marched from the Guildhall up Milsom Street, where to their delight they were showered with teleprinter punchings by postal workers on night shift. One crowd went down Southgate Street shouting, 'We want beer,' but all the refreshment they could get was mineral water from the fountain at the end of Bath Street.

Someone with an accordion appeared and to the strains of the music the people danced and sang and toasted each other in mineral water. One lorry, loaded with people – they must have infringed quite a few road regulations – stopped at the traffic lights in Westgate Street. Its occupants waited patiently for the lights to change, ringing hand bells the while. Much the same scenes were witnessed in other parts of the city, although the suburbs, for the most part, were quiet.

Many Bath people woke up this morning to find that peace had really arrived – and that it was raining! Women's thoughts were to get out quickly and do emergency shopping. Mere males just turned over and went to sleep again. In the city it was like a Friday or Saturday morning, the shops were full of people, and before 10 a.m. many women were returning home, their baskets loaded and arms full. There were queues at the butchers, the greengrocers, the cake shops and the newsagents.

Flags were springing up everywhere. Those on the Guildhall were hidden behind the parapet ready to be hoisted 'first thing' today. Colmer's Ltd, had a magnificent display. Union Street was like a Royal route. Milsom Street was a grand spectacle, too. Hawkers had been selling small flags several days before, so children were well supplied. Apart from the fact that there will be no buses for early workers tomorrow morning, the services will on both days be the same as any other Bank Holiday – that is a restricted service in the morning and full service later in the day.

Grocers' shops will be open till 1 p.m. tomorrow, but the Co-operative Society's food branches close at noon. All food shops will be expected to open for a few hours at least. Most of the leading restaurants will be shut on both days. Bath magistrates sat today (though the only defendant did not turn up) and they will sit again tomorrow if need be! The Band in the Gardens, the Theatre Royal, the Palace Theatre, Bath, and all the picture houses are carrying on as usual, thus adding to the gaiety of the occasion. The Red Aces will give a show in the park at 7 this evening and on both evenings the 'Victory Belles' will parade the city, giving a show at the Parade Gardens at 9.15 this evening and in the Park at 6.30 tomorrow night. There will be dances in the Pavilion both nights, and dancing in the Abbey Churchyard – an innovation. Flood lighting will illuminate all the principal buildings and landmarks.

A *Chronicle* correspondent, comparing the celebrations of the two Victory nights, observed:

There seems no doubt in our minds that V-E was by far the better. Something seemed to be lacking in V-J. Maybe it was because it followed so soon (surprisingly) after V-E; maybe it was because people had been out in the early hours of V-J Day after the midnight announcement and let off a lot of their steam then; maybe it was because little time was given to make adequate arrangements for bunfights; maybe it was because V-E lifted the air-raid terror from us – there are lots of 'maybes'. At any rate, V-J night didn't provide the thrills of V-E. That's just our opinion, mark you.

After some delay the Japanese surrender took effect on 18 August and was formalised on board the USS *Missouri* in Tokyo Bay on 2 September.

Home from the war: soldiers and sailors are among the happy guests at a children's street party to celebrate victory in Europe. This photograph was taken in Hanover Street.

In accepting the surrender on behalf of the Allies, America's General MacArthur expressed the hope that 'a better world would emerge out of the blood and carnage of the past'. Closer to home, the final word on the Second World War went to the *Chronicle*, which summed up the VJ-Day celebrations:

> For this was a night to remember to tell your children about. V-Days (and V-Nights) are great. But may the rest of our days – and theirs – be P-Days. And P stands for Peace!

CHAPTER 13

Bath's War Legacy

Nazi Germany was defeated and around her lay much of Europe in smoking ruins, pulverised into dust by a war that had cost the lives of millions. In the Far East, Japan's will to resist was crushed three months later by two atom bombs, heralding the dawn of a frightening new age of assured mutual annihilation by nuclear weapons, ten thousand times more destructive than anything that had gone before.

Bath's warrior sons returned home to 'Civvy Street', some after long periods of service at the war front, others from the often severe conditions of captivity in Germany and the Far East. They received no counselling to help them readjust to postwar life, but were expected just to 'get on with it'. Many children, only recently born when their fathers went off to war, did not recognise them on their return years later. Some men were plunged into further trauma when they

Children play on a bombsite at the west end of Julian Road and Rivers Street in the ruins of St Andrew's Church. Catharine Place can be seen in the distance in the gap between the houses. (Bath Reference Library)

discovered that their wives had been unfaithful to them during their enforced absence from home. Then there were the widows who would wait in vain for their menfolk to return from the war – men killed on land, at sea, and in the air. Theirs was a bitter-sweet taste of peace – a peace that their loved ones had fought so hard to secure, but the fruits of which they would never share.

After the euphoria of VE-Day and VJ-Day had evaporated, people began to face the stark reality of coming to terms with the brave new world of postwar Britain, with all its hopes and fears – hopes that the terrible suffering and sacrifice endured during six long years of conflict with a ruthless enemy would result, at last, in a stable and peaceful Europe; and the fears of adjusting to the, as yet, unknown demands of the new social order that was slowly beginning to emerge.

At home in Bath, the war had changed the face of the city forever. Before 1939, Bath had been not only a spa to which the better off had flocked in great numbers to take the 'cure', but also a city to which the wealthy had come to spend their declining years in the comfort and beautiful surroundings of the 'Queen City of the West'. The war was a great leveller. Never before had people from widely differing social backgrounds been encouraged to work shoulder to shoulder in the common cause of national survival. But such a situation did much to help break down social barriers in the postwar era.

Bath, the genteel resort of the well-to-do, was to change beyond recognition in the years following the war. Those who had enjoyed the luxury of domestic servants in prewar days found that the supply of willing labour for such work had largely dried up after 1945. Working-class girls had higher aspirations as a result of their war experiences. To be sure, private nursing homes for the elderly continued to flourish, but as the private incomes of their residents dwindled, gentlefolk came increasingly to depend on the provisions of the emerging Welfare State.

Two events that occurred after the outbreak of war – one demographic, the other physical – had made lasting impressions on the character of the city. These were the transfer to Bath of Admiralty personnel from London in 1939, and the devastating *Baedeker* blitz of 1942.

With the arrival of large numbers of Admiralty staff in the city, a severe strain was placed on accommodation. The temporary influx of evacuees and war workers exacerbated the problem. Hotels were commandeered for use as offices and for the same purpose groups of prefab 'hutments' sprang up on the heights of Ensleigh and Foxhill, and along the Warminster Road. Three of the most prestigious hotels appropriated by the Admiralty in the city centre never reverted to their former use: they were the Grand Pump Room (demolished in the 1960s), the Pulteney and the Empire (both converted into apartments).

While the 'vackees' and war workers eventually returned to their homes, the Admiralty departments and their staff became a permanent presence in the city. The unemployment situation in Bath of the 1930s was eased to some extent by the presence of the Admiralty, which was able to offer residents temporary clerical jobs some of which were extended well into the postwar years.

The unanticipated blitz in April 1942 brought Bath residents and visitors temporarily into the front line of war, with considerable loss of life and property. Miraculously, in the heart of the city the Abbey, Roman Baths, Pump Room and Guildhall were not hit in the bombing, but the recently restored Assembly

Rooms and several historic houses, including the Elizabethan Abbey Church House, were severely damaged and had to be rebuilt. Three churches, St Andrew's, St James's and Holy Trinity, and one chapel, All Saints', of which only the shells remained, were later demolished. Certain areas of the city were so badly damaged during the blitz that the only course of action was to redesign and rebuild completely.

But the postwar redevelopment of Bath was spasmodic and took some time to get underway. Well into the 1960s many bomb sites could still be seen across the city, the overgrown and unsightly legacies of a recent but violent wartime past. Bath's postwar planners did not seem to spend time studying designs that would be sympathetic to this great Georgian city. Indeed, the replacement structures sanctioned by Bath's postwar planners were later described by Professor Barry Cunliffe as little more than 'acts of vandalism'. His words on the matter are worthy of quotation:

> Hundreds and hundreds of eighteenth and early nineteenth century buildings, mainly artisan dwellings, were bulldozed flat irrespective of the fact that many of them were listed as buildings of note under the Town and Country Planning Act of 1947. What many people today would regard as successive acts of vandalism were proposed, debated, and approved by the Local Planning Authority with the support of the elected representatives. No laws were broken, no corners cut – it was the democratic process at work deliberately modifying Bath in a way which seemed to those in power to be in the best interests of the community. When the City Architect said 'If you want to keep Georgian artisans' houses, then you'll have to find Georgian artisans to live in them' we can only suppose that he genuinely believed that restoration and renovation were not viable alternatives to demolition and rebuilding.

It is a tragedy that Bath has been ruined by the erection of some buildings that can only be described as hideous and totally incongruous. What the Luftwaffe started in 1942, Bath's postwar planners certainly finished.

One of the happier events to come out of the Second World War was the twinning of Bath with the Dutch town of Alkmaar, a link that can actually be traced back as far as the beginning of the war. At that time a Bath Rotarian, Mr F.C. ('Jimmy') Wills, was head warden of A Group in Bath's Civil Defence Service. One of his part-time wardens was Eli Prins, a young schoolmaster and member of a well-known Alkmaar family who had escaped from Holland in the face of the merciless German Blitzkrieg in 1940. Eli came to stay in Bath, where his sister and English brother-in-law were living.

After hearing from Eli of the terrible starvation and suffering that the Germans and the war had brought to the people of Alkmaar, Bath Rotary Club decided to do what it could to arrange for gifts of clothes and tools, and 'of anything that could be spared, to be put in store until the day of Holland's liberation'. Shortly after the Bath blitz in 1942, 'Jimmy' Wills suggested Bath should 'adopt' Alkmaar and the idea was put to the Netherlands' Queen-in-exile, Wilhelmina, who approved. As a result the Bath–Alkmaar Adoption Appeal Committee was set up in 1945.

These Bath children were among those on the first exchange between the city and Alkmaar in 1946. The boy in the centre is Gordon Banks. (Gordon Banks)

An Alkmaar Week, which ran from 23 to 28 July 1945, met with a hearty response from the citizens of Bath. Despite suffering themselves from the privations of war and the continued rationing of clothes and foodstuffs, Bathonians donated over 45,000 articles of clothing and over £7,500 was collected. A further £1,000 was collected on the streets of Bath as a result of Saturday afternoon 'tours' with a barrel organ painted in the Dutch national colours. This additional sum was earmarked for the purchase of a new English section at the Alkmaar Library to replace the one destroyed by the Germans.

As part of the fund-raising activities in Alkmaar Week, a ball was held at the Pump Room. In attendance were representatives of the Netherlands government and armed forces, and the Burgomaster of Alkmaar, Jonkheer F.H. van Kinschot, who was flown over specially for the event in an aircraft of the US Army Air Force. Later, the Burgomaster presented the Honorary Freedom of Alkmaar to the Mayor of Bath, the first time such an honour had been bestowed on a foreigner. A return visit was soon arranged for representatives of Bath to join in the Dutch town's liberation festivities, which proved to be a very moving experience for all concerned. But behind all the Dutch joy of being free again lay the terrible destruction and desolation, privation and starvation suffered over five years of German occupation.

Headstones at Haycombe Cemetery of some of the four hundred Bath residents who were killed in the air raids of 1942. (Authors)

Once contact had been established, arrangements were made for the reception in Bath of fifty Alkmaar children in October 1945 and it was not long before regular exchanges between the two cities were being made. Alkmaar presented Bath with a fine copper gong, used to summon the City Council to order, and Bath reciprocated by presenting to the Alkmaar Museum the barrel organ that had raised £1,000 during Alkmaar Week. The link has remained strong and fruitful ever since and to commemorate the fiftieth anniversary of the twinning, celebrations were held in both cities during 1995.

In the Bath of the late 1990s there is little to remind one of the Second World War, or of the suffering and deprivation endured by the city's inhabitants during those desperate years. Bath is now a prosperous city where the 'here and now' are very much to the fore, and to many people the past consists only of the Roman Baths and the Georgian crescents. When you next visit the Pump Room or Pavilion think of the thousands of people, young and old, who more

Lest we forget: memorial tablet at Haycombe Cemetery bearing the inscription '1939–1945 THIS TABLET MARKS THE GRAVES OF THOSE WHO DIED IN BATH DURING THE AIR RAIDS ON 25TH 26TH 27TH APRIL 1942'. A Book of Remembrance recording the names and addresses of all those who died is preserved in Bath Abbey. (Authors)

Bombed sites were still to be seen for many years after the war. This was Hanover Terrace, Kensington.

The old Labour Exchange in James Street West remains as a mute testimony to the violence of the blitz. Its walls still bear the pock-marks of aircraft cannon shells and bomb shrapnel. (Authors)

than half a century ago danced the wartime nights away to forget their troubles, but privately fearing the outcome of the war. Next time you drive past the gates of Haycombe Cemetery, think also of Bath's four hundred blitz dead who lie within, and of their families who mourn them still. Visit their graves and witness the fresh flowers that are still placed before them, memories of mother or daughter, brother or husband, undimmed with the passage of more than fifty years. Walk along James Street West and put your fingers into the deep shrapnel pock-marks in the stone walls of the old Labour Exchange building. They are probably the most tangible legacy of the Second World War that, for Bath and its inhabitants, was arguably 'the best of times, the worst of times'.

Bibliography

PUBLISHED SECONDARY SOURCES

1. Books

Calder, A. *The People's War: Britain 1939–45* (London, Jonathan Cape, 1969)

Gardner, J. *The People's War* (London, Collins & Brown, 1991)

Hawkins, M. *Somerset at War 1939–1945* (Wimborne, The Dovecote Press, 1988)

Kohn, Dr F. *It Went Through My Mind* (privately published, *c.* 1979)

Lee, E. *1939–1945: Evacuation to Bath – The Evacuation of Admiralty Staff to Bath* (Bath City Council, n.d.)

Lloyd, J. *The Royal United Hospital, Bath: A Short History* (Bristol, Redcliffe Press, 1982)

Longmate, N. *The Real Dad's Army* (London, Arrow Books, 1974)

Mitchell, P. *Chariots of the Sea* (Huddersfield, Richard Netherwood Ltd, 1998)

Ramsey, Winston G. *The Battle of Britain Then and Now* (London, Battle of Britain Prints International, 1985)

——. *The Blitz Then and Now* (3 vols) (London, Battle of Britain Prints International, 1987)

Rothnie, N. *The Baedeker Blitz: Hitler's Attack on Britain's Historic Cities* (Shepperton, Ian Allan, 1992)

Shores, C. and Williams, C. *Aces High* (London, Grub Street, 1994)

2. Newspapers

Bath and Wilts Chronicle and Herald, Daily Telegraph

UNPUBLISHED SECONDARY SOURCES

Penny, John. 'Bath: The Most Devastating Baedeker Blitz – Luftwaffe Efficiency of Defensive Failure During the Raids of 1942?' (MA Dissertation, Bath Spa University College, 1998)

In Bath of the late 1990s there are few reminders of the Second World War, or of the suffering endured during those desperate years. (Authors)

Items should be returned to the library from which they
were borrowed on or before the date stamped above,
unless a renewal has been granted.   LM6.108.5

Wiltshire
COUNTY COUNCIL
LIBRARY & MUSEUM SERVICE

BYTHESEA
ROAD   TROWBRIDGE